The Milford Series
POPULAR WRITERS OF TODAY
Volume Thirty-Eight
ISSN 0163-2469

THE MAGIC LABYRINTH OF
PHILIP JOSE'FARMER

Edgar L. Chapman

R. Reginald

The Borgo Press

San Bernardino, California
MCMLXXXIV

For Margaret, who cared, and for Ben and Terry

ACKNOWLEDGMENTS

Thanks to Charles Clancy, Warren Dwyer, Dennis McInerny, Carol Maier, Dean Max Kele, Tom Kent, George Scheetz, Mary T. Brizzi, Patricia Mc-Carney, Julie and Diana Cutt, Professor Richard Chapman, Professor Josiah Carberry, and especially to Phil Farmer himself, for his friendship and encouragement.

CONTENTS

813.54

C36m

145447

nw.1988

Library of Congress Cataloging in Publication Data:

Chapman, Edgar L., 1936-
     The magic labyrinth of Philip Jose Farmer.

    (The Milford series : popular writers of today ; v. 38)
    Bibliography: p.
    1. Farmer, Philip Jose—Criticism and interpretation. I. Title. II. Series.
PS3556.A72Z62   813'.54   81-21603
ISBN 0-89370-158-0 (cloth, $11.95)
ISBN 0-89370-258-7 (paper; $4.95)

Produced, designed, and published by R. Reginald and Mary A. Burgess, The Borgo Press, P.O. Box 2845, San Bernardino, CA 92406, USA. Cover design by Michael Pastucha.

First Edition---December, 1984

Introduction

Philip Jose Farmer, like many other science fiction and fantasy authors, might be considered, in traditional literary terms, a romantic living in a century when the official and accepted literary mode of the novel is "realism." Northrop Frye, a brilliant critic of the romance, has suggested in his study, *The Secular Scripture*, that "the rise of science fiction" in recent years has been the symptom of a widespread revival of interest in the sophisticated romance. Whatever the reasons for the contemporary popularity of science fiction—or speculative fiction, as some would have it—Farmer's career has paralleled the progress of the genre from the fifties through the seventies in its growth from a cult enthusiasm or a literary ghetto to public acceptance.

Before taking a brief overview of Farmer's career, a glance at his life and background will prove helpful. Some of the facts of Farmer's biography are fairly well known, having become a part of science fiction folklore; but they have frequently been subject to distortion and inaccuracy.

Farmer was born in North Terre Haute, Indiana, in January 1918, the oldest of five children. Farmer's father was an electrical power engineer, of Scotch, Irish, Anglo-Saxon, Welsh, and perhaps Indian forebears. Both parents were practicing Christian Scientists. Originally, Farmer's middle name was simply Jose, the first name of his father's mother, and a cognomen Farmer detested.

For the first four years of Farmer's life, the Farmer family moved often, residing in Indianapolis; in Greenwood, Indiana; on a farm near Mexico, Missouri; and finally settling in Peoria, Illinois, in 1922. Peoria proved to be Farmer's permanent home for more than the next three decades. Farmer attended Columbia Junior High School and Peoria Central High School. While studying high school Spanish, Farmer altered his middle name to Jose, thereby expressing his independence.

Farmer was eager to attain a higher education, but the path to a college degree proved to be a long and arduous one, for he graduated from high school into the world of the Great Depression. He attended the University of Missouri at Columbia briefly in 1936, and for a semester in 1939; in between, he tried Bradley Polytechnic Institute (now Bradley University) in Peoria in 1938-39. After trying various odd jobs in Peoria, Farmer began working in 1941 for Keystone Steel and Wire in Bartonville, a town adjoining Peoria; and he continued there, except for a brief interruption for military service in 1942, until 1952. In 1941, Farmer married Bette Virginia Andre; two children, a son and a daughter, arrived during the war years, making Farmer's hopes for a university degree more remote. Farmer persevered, however, going to

3

night school at Bradley in the late forties, and with the help of the G.I. Bill in 1949-50, when he combined a 48-hour work week with a heavy academic load, finally achieved his goal. He was awarded a B.S. in English from Bradley in 1950.

During his Bradley years, Farmer benefited from the instruction of three able teachers in the English Department: Bennett Hollowell, Sue Maxwell, and Olive B. White. The three came from excellent graduate schools and were dedicated teachers whose presence counteracted much of the provincial atmosphere that Peoria seemed to exude in those days. Though none of the three had published very widely, partly due to the heavy teaching loads they carried, they were professors of wide and bracing erudition. Olive White, the sister of Helen White, a distinguished scholar at University of Wisconsin, merits particular attention for her exceptionally literate historical novels about the English Renaissance. Such instructors were an encouragement to a young man's ambitions to become an author.

Like many budding novelists, Farmer showed a youthful interest in poetry, and actually published some verse in the forties. But eventually he turned to prose, and then to science fiction, for reasons that receive discussion later. With the sale of the novelette version of "The Lovers" in 1952 to *Startling Stories*, Farmer made an impressive debut; the story gained him the Hugo award as the most promising newcomer to science fiction for 1952. During succeeding years, Farmer sold many other short stories and novelettes, but his first real effort to establish himself as a full-time writer and novelist produced the greatest disappointment of his career.

When Shasta Publishers sponsored a contest for the best science fiction novel by a first novelist, Farmer quit his job and worked at high speed to produce the lengthy novel, *River of Eternity* (or, *I Owe for the Flesh*, Farmer's title), the first version of Farmer's Riverworld epic. Shasta declared Farmer the winner, with supposed publication of the cloth book to follow and the paperback to be issued by Pocket Books. But Shasta failed to provide the advance money it had promised, and simultaneously began asking for some maddening revisions of the work; finally, in 1954, Shasta declared bankruptcy, thus ending any obligations to Farmer.

Farmer suffered serious financial and emotional reverses from this defeat that scarred much of his early career. The Riverworld novel seemed unpublishable, since few hardcover publishers were issuing science fiction novels in the fifties. Farmer resumed working at various jobs in Peoria, while writing stories in his spare time. In 1956, Farmer finally left Peoria, to take a job as a technical writer for General Electric in Syracuse, New York; and this profession sustained Farmer through the next decade and a half, while he continued to write in his spare time.

During Farmer's years as a technical writer, Farmer and his family lived a rather nomadic existence. Two years in Syracuse were followed by five years in Scottsdale, Arizona, as a Motorola employee. Then there was a brief stint in Ann Arbor, Michigan, another year in Phoenix, and finally a job for McDonnell-Douglas in Southern California in 1965. This employment lasted until June, 1969, shortly before the moon landing, when, ironically, there were large layoffs in the aerospace industry. Farmer took this opportunity to gamble again on a career as a full-time writer. He published five novels in 1970, and has never had to look back.

In October of 1970, Farmer moved back to Peoria with his family, where he has been something of a celebrity, and one of the more distinguished citizens of the central Illinois town where he grew up.

Farmer's career has gradually changed over four decades of professional writing. Although his first stories appeared in the forties, the first significant work was published in the fifties, with the novelette version of "The Lovers" and other early stories establishing Farmer as an iconoclastic flailer against societal dogmas and taboos, particularly those concerning sex and religion. Hostility to his liberal attitudes and Farmer's frustration over the unpublished Riverworld book made the fifties a decade of struggle.

In the sixties Farmer enjoyed greater success, beginning with the novel version of *The Lovers* in 1961, and continuing with such novels as *Inside Outside, Night of Light*, and *Flesh*. As interest in science fiction and fantasy grew during the decade, Farmer consolidated his status as a professional by writing adventure science fiction, especially the successful "World of Tiers" series for Ace Books. By the end of the decade, Farmer's perserverance was beginning to pay off in increased public and critical recognition. The story, "Riders of the Purple Wage," published in 1967, and the first published Riverworld novel, *To Your Scattered Bodies Go* (1971), both garnered awards.

In the seventies and eighties, Farmer's output has been prodigious, the long-delayed flowering of the talent that shone with such bright promise in the fifties. During this period, Farmer published his Tarzan and Doc Savage "biographies," and many other books relating to the mythos surrounding the pair. Five Riverworld novels, now re-conceived by a mature imagination, were written, including the memorable *The Dark Design* (1977) and the widely praised *The Magic Labyrinth* (published in 1980 but completed in 1979). Farmer also produced his celebrated—some say infamous—parody of Kurt Vonnegut, *Venus on the Half-Shell*, by "Kilgore Trout," and many impressive short stories. Also published during this period was a new work of the Tiers series, *The Lavalite World*, and the inauguration of a new adventure series, the Opar novels. Finally, a number of thought-provoking novels not belonging to any series were also published, including *Jesus on Mars*, and the highly impressive *Dark Is the Sun*. As Farmer entered the decade of the eighties, he was at the height of his powers; and the fame, recognition, and public acceptance that had been so slow in coming were at last within his grasp.

Obviously, Farmer's career has benefited from the freedom to write full time during the seventies. Clearly, too, much of Farmer's work has become more acceptable as a result of the sexual and social revolutions of the sixties. But just as clearly, Farmer's career has flowered concurrently with the growing public interest in science fiction and fantasy during the 1970s. The causes for this new fascination with fantastic literature are not easy to define, but some can be suggested: the success of Tolkien's Trilogy with the mass audience; the revival of Edgar Rice Burroughs's novels; the presence of a science fiction writer, Kurt Vonnegut, speaking through his satire to a younger generation disillusioned with war and social hypocrisy; the realization that technological and social changes long imagined by science fiction writers are finally coming into reality; and so forth.

Perhaps Frye's contention that the public has returned to "sophisticated romance" following the decline of realistic fiction is the best explanation for the phenomenon. This is a literary form that can be both satirical and exploratory, and leads, for Frye and other critics, to the creation of new myths and the remaking, or perhaps the visionary restatement, of old myths. Such purposes are certainly central to Farmer's work, if not to all of fantastic literature.

Before proceeding to a detailed study of Farmer's work, we should note that science fiction, although it developed its own conventions in the twentieth century (particularly in pulp magazines), descends at least in part from the tradition of the literary romance, particularly the quest romance, a favorite form of the nineteenth century romantic poets, and later of such adventure writers as H. Rider Haggard. Farmer makes three well-known writers characters in his Riverworld novels, and each of them was something of a romantic, whose best-known works draw on the tradition of the nineteenth-century quest romance: Mark Twain, Jack London, and Richard Burton. Of course, this statement must be qualified by the fact that Twain considered himself a realist, enjoying a very ambivalent relationship at best with the romantic tradition, even if *Huckleberry Finn* is often a picaresque parody of romance conventions. Similarly, it is worth noting that Richard Burton's quest narratives are not fiction in the usual sense, but more or less factual accounts of his explorations, of which Burton was the quest hero. Nevertheless, these three precursors have clearly influenced Farmer, so that some possible parallels between Farmer and these writers can be drawn.

To compare Farmer to Twain may seem surprising, but there is clear evidence of Farmer's interest in and admiration for this classic American writer. Like Twain, Farmer grew up in the Midwest near a great river; like Twain, Farmer was somewhat alienated from the community's canons of virtue; like Twain, Farmer lived something of a struggling, nomadic life before establishing himself as a writer, although Farmer has hardly been the world traveler that Twain was. Farmer has the benefit of a college degree, but there is a sense in which Farmer, driven by a boundless curiosity about the world, is a self-educated man. Like Twain, too, Farmer has a broad sense of humor with its roots set deep in folklore, as well as a talent for comedy and satire; although Farmer is hardly an acknowledged genius with celebrity status, as Twain was in his own time.

One of the major reasons for Farmer's identification with Twain is a certain similarity of attitudes and themes. Twain satirized hypocrisy, greed, religious bigotry, provincialism, social pretension, and racism, targets also of Farmer's satire. But these parallels should not be pressed too far. They are meant to be merely suggestive. Farmer's reputation, though distinguised in his genre, is not to be compared with the literary eminence of Twain, or at present even with that of Kurt Vonnegut, whom Farmer admires as a twentieth-century iconoclast in the Twain tradition. But Farmer's choice of working in an unheralded popular genre is comparable to Twain's career as a popular humorist in at least one respect: neither was initially taken seriously by contemporary literary critics.

If Farmer was influenced by Twain, and shares some qualities with him, there are also affinities between Farmer and Jack London, another character in the Riverworld novels. Farmer, like London, rose from a struggling family in an obscure working class setting; Farmer also exhibits proletarian sympathies sometimes in conflict with his admiration for aristocratic individualism.

Farmer does share London's belief in socialism, but both authors may be described as largely self-educated liberals who succeeded by hard work and strong wills. Both Farmer and London are attracted to the noble savage and the heroic superman figures, conceived as products of vitalist evolutionary development: London has his romanticized Eskimos and Indians and his Wolf Larsen; Farmer has his Amerindian heroes and his Tarzan archetypes. Again, like London, Farmer has a speculative mind almost complusively interested in testing ideas in fiction, and thinks of himself more as a disciplined professional than as a serious "artist." London and Farmer both excel as adventure novelists. Interestingly enough, London experimented with science fiction, which was just developing as a genre in his time, while Farmer has often inclined to describe and invent "primitive" life styles and values in his science fiction. Both London and Farmer, in fact, are mythmakers who celebrate primitive worlds; it is thus not surprising that Farmer has edited a collection of London short stories.

Although Twain and London offer interesting parallels to Farmer, it is no secret that Richard Burton, the nineteenth-century English explorer and man of letters, is one of Farmer's personal heroes. Burton is the most important figure in the Riverworld epic, and Farmer has indicated that his characterization of Burton is partly a compensation for his frustrated desire to write Burton's biography. This fascination with Burton points to some important characteristics in Farmer's work. Burton was a persistent explorer, not simply in the geographical sense, but in the realm of culture and anthropology. His life was a series of encounters with other cultures, including the Asian Indian, the East African, Islam, and Brigham Young's Mormonism. This restless and compulsive interest in other societies may have developed out of Burton's rebellion against the puritanism and narrowness of Victorian England, but it was also the mark of genuine intellectual curiosity. Like Burton, Farmer's work shows a belligerent rejection of sexual prudery, a salient feature of the Peoria culture Farmer knew in his youth, and a dominant aspect of American society from the nineteenth century to the 1950s. Farmer's work often describes societies that are sexually liberated, or at any rate ruled by different customs than middle class Anglo-Saxon morals. Thus far, the parallel is obvious, but Burton's influence on Farmer can also be seen by noting Farmer's interest in Sufi mysticism, which was first brought to his attention by Burton's writing.

Burton's life in many ways has probably had greater influence on Farmer than Burton's writing, although Farmer has certainly read the Englishman's work. Burton's life is a paradigm of the seeker who values experience for its own sake; his sheer lust for adventure and for a constant renewal of experience has surely struck a responsive chord in Farmer. Other Farmer heroes, like Kickaha, with their sheer joy in adventure, may also owe something to Burton's example.

These parallels define certain features of Farmer's work, but there is another point worth making here: Farmer has been influenced strongly by literary forces and figures outside the science fiction genre. To the names already mentioned we may add D. H. Lawrence, James Joyce, and Robert Graves, all influences occasionally detectable in Farmer's fiction. Lawrence and Joyce have surely contributed to Farmer's iconoclastic concern with sexual taboos—one celebrated Farmer story also uses Joycean puns. The presence of Graves's poetic mythology of the "white goddess" or triumphant feminine principle is an important force throughout Farmer's fiction, from *The Lovers* to the Opar novels and the last Riverworld volume. In short, Farmer's work displays his omnivorous taste for all forms of literature.

At the same time, however, Farmer's roots within the science fiction genre should not be overlooked. As the readers of Lord Greystoke's genealogy in *Tarzan Alive* know, Farmer displays a formidable acquaintance with the pulp heroes of the twenties and thirties. The "biographies" of Tarzan and Doc Savage pay a tongue-in-cheek homage to this tradition, which, whatever its absurdities, richly stimulated the imagination of its readers. Farmer also shows his indebtedness to the science fiction of the "Golden Age," the era of John W. Campbell, Jr., who became Editor of *Astounding Science Fiction* in 1938 and soon began to encourage more intelligent uses of science and more credible narrative conventions. In the forties, such writers as Isaac Asimov and Robert A. Heinlein, prompted by Campbell, began to develop a much more sophisticated science fiction than anything yet seen in the pulps. The Campbell era, which continued until the sixties, was the "classic age" of "hard science fiction," emphasizing logical extrapolation, rationalized technology, and plausible characterizations. Of course, from our perspective, the Campbell age seems somewhat less rationalistic and realistic than it appeared to contemporaries. No doubt its links to the era of thirties pulp romance are stronger than many have thought.

Nevertheless, to a young rising author like Farmer, desirous of reaching the popular audience while voicing liberal social criticism, the science fiction genre in the forties must have seemed exciting and provocative, offering an opportunity for successful commercial writing wedding formulaic conventions to intellectual themes. Here one could express criticism about religious bigotry, racism, sexual taboos, and self-righteousness more readily than almost anywhere else in American society. And Philip Jose Farmer was never bashful about expressing his beliefs.

I
The Romantic Rebel

(1)

The Lovers, published in a novelette version in *Startling Stories* in 1952, then as a novel in 1961, was Farmer's first important success in both forms; it remains one of Farmer's most widely read books. Both versions of the story created the reputation of Farmer as a daring innovator, whose favorite theme was a liberal view of sexual relationships. In retrospect, the book now seems less radical than it did in the fifties or early sixties; but we are now on the other side of a public shift in attitudes about sex and its treatment in popular fiction, films, and television drama. In the age of television melodrama like *Dallas*, it may be hard to recall the cultural mood of the early Eisenhower era. Then, sexual liaisons without benefit of clergy appeared mainly in "serious" novels, the work of Mickey Spillane and his imitators, or in the romanticized historical novels of Frank Yerby and Edison Marshall—certainly not in science fiction. Robert Heinlein's *Stranger in a Strange Land*, published in 1961, the same year as the novelized version of *The Lovers* and almost a decade after its magazine appearance, was considered shockingly innovative for the field. Yet *Stranger in a Strange Land* is certainly no stronger in its impact than *The Lovers* (nor is it as skillfully crafted or as credible), and *Stranger* was the first indication that Heinlein held "advanced" sexual views. Leslie Fiedler aptly described the importance of *The Lovers* and other early Farmer stories when he commented, in a laudatory review of *Tarzan Alive* in the *Los Angeles Times* (April 23, 1972), that "Philip Farmer was, however, during the 50's, the only major writer of science fiction to deal *explicitly* with sex."

If, in the perspective of a later decade, *The Lovers* seems rather less revolutionary, it remains a rebellious dystopian romance, asserting in a rather belligerent way its attitude of "the world well lost" for erotic passion. Two features of the novel are especially striking. First, there is the vivid and original relationship between a naive human male and an alien woman; and secondly, there is the satirical portrait of the repressed conformist society that opposes the lovers. The second point should not be overlooked at the expense of the first: *The Lovers* is a solid dystopian novel, one of the better ones to emerge from the popular American science fiction tradition. Clearly influenced by Huxley's *Brave New World* and Orwell's *1984*, *The Lovers* follows their tradition of opposing an erotic relationship to a dehumanized and dehumanizing tyranny (although in Huxley the erotic relationship is frustrated by the woman's inability to understand the Savage's ideal of romantic love). Other influences here include D. H. Lawrence and Robert Graves. Although *The Lovers* lacks the philosophical maturity of Huxley and Orwell, the novel does not suffer by comparison with such SF dystopias as Heinlein's "If This Goes On..." (1940), Frederik Pohl and C. M. Kornbluth's *The Space Merchants* (1953), or Bradbury's *Fahrenheit 451* (1953). Indeed, the artistry of Farmer's novel is fairly well accomplished, despite some beginner's flaws, for at this point Farmer lacks Huxley's command of irony or Lawrence's skill at characterizing women in erotic relationships.

The Lovers is set in an imaginatively conceived social tyranny, one of Farmer's more impressive extrapolated societies. The time is 3026 A.D., when a biological war has devastated most of America and Europe, although a civilization carrying on some debased Western traditions still exists in Hawaii, Japan, Canada, and Iceland. Locked in a cold war with the Israeli Republic, the Haijac Union is a police state that enforces conformity to the Sturch, or state church, an unholy fusion of religious and political authority whose theocratic principles are a shrewd synthesis of puritanism, Freudianism, and behaviorism.

The alleged founder or Forerunner of the Sturch, whose name is constantly invoked as an authority symbol, is Isaac Sigmen whose name suggests vague Old Testament overtones as well as a combination of Newton and Freud. Newton, a great physicist and a conservative Christian, developed a physics that provided an eighteenth-century world view supporting both Christianity and deism, and a static social order. Freud, though an agnostic and an iconoclast for much of his life, erected his psychoanalytic theories into a dogma of the kind attractive to authoritarians, whether social reformers, dictators, or literary critics. At any rate, Farmer, in making Sigmen the father symbol of his dystopia, is probably adopting the strategy of Huxley, who made "Our Ford" (a fusion of Freud and Ford) the founder of his brave new world.

Farmer follows the example of both Orwell and Huxley in depicting the way a powerful government seeks to corrupt language by coopting words for its own purposes. Not only are old religious formulas revised in accordance with the sacred name of Sigmen (as in Huxley), but proverbs have been rewritten to make apparent injustice seem synonymous with reason, as in *1984*. For instance, Farmer's hero quotes a famous saying attributed to the "Forerunner": "All men are brothers, though some are more favored by the father than others." Perhaps the most significant abuse of language is the kidnapping of the words "real" and "reality" to refer to whatever the Sturch considers desirable. Individualism thus becomes "unreal" behavior.

Farmer does not develop this theme of language corruption quite as thoroughly as Orwell does in *1984*. Rather, Farmer tends to subordinate depiction of his dystopian society to his narrative, which concerns the awkward struggle of Farmer's naive hero, Hal Yarrow, to find a different life from that his society wants for him.

Despite some rebellious feelings, Yarrow at first is in many ways a puritanical young man who wants to be successful by pleasing his superiors. This type of hero appears in many of Farmer's early stories: an innocent young idealist, frequently a victim of social conditioning. In the middle years of Farmer's career, this naive figure tends to disappear, being replaced by the trickster hero, but he returns in Farmer's late, important work, *Dark Is the*

Sun (1979).

Yarrow's resistance to his world provides some internal drama in the novel, but his feelings of revolt are ambivalent and indecisive in the early scenes. His conventional marriage to a timid wife causes considerable conflict: even more sexually repressed than Yarrow, Mary also lacks his sense of humor. Although Farmer could have portrayed her a bit more compassionately, her timidity and lack of imagination are exasperating. Yarrow impatiently accuses her of maddening intellectual naivete: "The trouble with you, Mary, is that you're absolutely literal-minded. Don't you know that the Forerunner himself didn't demand that his prescriptions be taken literally? He himself said that circumstances sometimes warranted modifications!"

In Yarrow's marriage sexual intercourse and conception exist, but they are considered joyless duties performed on behalf of the state. Although Yarrow chafes under these restraints, his rebellious feelings mainly find an outlet through jokes, sarcasm, and inner reservations. Even though more liberal than his wife, he does not completely reject the teachings of the Forerunner or the imperatives of his bureaucratic superiors. In short, Yarrow is effectively characterized as a dissatisfied young man on the verge of rebellion with his resistance blocked by a will to conform, until he is given the opportunity for a personal quest for freedom and sexual liberation.

Dystopian novels usually center on the gradual movement of the hero away from socially accepted opinions toward illicit secret resistance groups, paralled by an intellectual journey which is prompted by the discovery of forbidden books. Huxley's Savage in *Brave New World*, though a lonely rebel, has his proscribed Shakespeare to inspire him; and Bradbury's fireman in *Fahrenheit 451* finds various literary classics to open his eyes to other possibilities. Similarly, Yarrow is a linguist whose occupation gives him access to forgotten or censored books: his reading includes the "unexpurgated Milton," with its references to Greek mythology, as opposed to the official *Revised and Real Milton*. Yarrow's profession also keeps him from being easily influenced by government propaganda; as a linguist, Yarrow is aware of the power of language, yet less susceptible than most to the magic or tyranny that words can exert.

Afraid that his occasional nonconformity will be punished, Yarrow instead is given a dramatic opportunity to change his life by joining a secret interstellar expedition. Yarrow's release from his confining job and stultifying marriage leads to the central drama in the novel. By becoming the linguist on a voyage to Ozagen, a planet forty years distant, Yarrow is allowed to divorce his wife, although divorce is forbidden by the Sturch. Here and elsewhere Farmer makes a satirical thrust at the facility by which religious establishments bend the teachings of their scriptures whenever the need arises.

Yarrow's liberation begins with his trip into space, for, despite spending most of it in suspended animation, he devotes several months to working on a grammar of the Siddo language, the tongue of one of the two dominant nations of Ozagen. Such independent work stimulates Yarrow's desire for more freedom.

Ozagen, the scene of the final two-thirds of the book, provides a pastoral contrast to the rigid classes and overcrowded industrialization of the Haijac. "Ozagen" is no accidental evocation of Oz; the planet was named by its discoverer "Oz again." Siddo, the capital, is laid out like a gigantic park; this Arcadian atmosphere represents a world of natural fertility preferable to the sterile gloom of Yarrow's Earth. The dominant Ozagenians are highly evolved and sentient insectoid creatures, whose tranquil society contains many attractive features. Ozagen technology, even in Siddo, putters along at the level of the early twentieth century, a slow-paced period before the First World War when cars and airplanes were simpler and more eccentric than to-day (a nostalgia for this more innocent technology appears again in the River-world novels).

Yarrow's colleagues on the expedition are portrayed satirically, as their society on earth has been. Feeling vast contempt for the Ozagenians, they scornfully call them "wogglebugs" (another allusion from Frank Baum's works, of which Farmer is very fond), and plan to exterminate them when convenient to clear the planet for colonists from Earth. However, the terres-trials pretend friendship for the Ozagenians, temporarily restrained by the prudent desire to discover whether their hosts have any advanced secret weapons. In his portrait of human ethnocentrism, Farmer follows a familiar science fiction tradition by satirizing the way a technologically advanced so-ciety treats those whose capacity to make war is inferior. This theme appears in science fiction at least as early as C. S. Lewis's *Out of the Silent Planet* (1938) with its satirical portraits of Weston and Devine, who want to turn Mars into a colony for Western culture and its technology.

After evoking the pastoral world of Ozagen, Farmer introduces a heroine who fuses two mythic archetypes: the "lost race" motif and the "fatal" or daimonic woman of romantic tradition, potent symbols in fantasy and science fiction from the time of H. Rider Haggard, Edgar Rice Burroughs, and H. G. Wells. Both archetypes, which are vividly portrayed in Haggard's *She*, are legacies from Romanticism, which in turn inherited them from such sources as Samuel Johnson's *Rasselas* and the great imaginative works of the Renaissance.

More important than the sources of the archetypes is their meaning. The "lost race" theme usually embodies the discovery or re-discovery of a people more primitive, innocent, and virtuous than "civilized" humanity, often found in some hidden valley or on a remote plateau. Lost race stories normal-ly carry overtones of the earthly paradise or the recovery of a lost Eden and forgotten innocence. Of course, such earthly paradises may either be genu-ine, as with Lothlorien in J.R.R. Tolkien's *Lord of the Rings*, or sinister and treacherous, such as the "Bower of Bliss" in Edmund Spenser's *The Faerie Queene*, and the Valley of the Blind in Wells's "In the Country of the Blind." In *The Lovers* Farmer uses the Ozian and Arcadian imagery to suggest an Edenic mood, but the presence of the daimonic woman figure adds ambigu-ous connotations.

The daimonic woman, a heroine who offers a transcendent but forbidden love to the hero, is often associated with the lost race archetype; she may be a figure who brings authentic fulfillment, or be revealed as a sinister temptress who liberates the hero from a conventional life, only to cause undeserved suf-fering. John Keats's "La Belle Dame Sans Merci" provides a brief descrip-tion of the "the fatal woman" in her demonic aspect.

Yarrow's fatal woman belongs to a lost species resembling mankind (al-though we eventually learn that they are insectoid); he discovers the "lali-tha" while investigating some ruins. Survivors of a war with Ozagen's domi-nant species, the lalitha worship a deification of the feminine principle whose power is a major theme of Farmer's fiction. Yarrow's woman, curiously, has a vaguely Gallic personality, being named Jeannette Rastignac, and speaking a quaint version of French, with minor changes attributable to the passage of a thousand years. Jeannette's French personality is explained away somewhat awkwardly as the result of a father descended from a group of Quebec French who emigrated from Earth in the past.

Jeannette is extraordinarily beautiful and knows the art of applying cosmetics (forbidden on Earth); Yarrow takes her to his apartment in the city of Siddo, and they soon embark on a torrid affair. Jeannette is an accomplished mistress: "His wife and he had remained outside the circle of each other, but Jeannette knew the geometry that would take him in and the chemistry that would mix his substance with hers." It is one of the weaknesses of the novel, however, that Farmer's writing—as this passage illustrates—does not always convey satisfactorily the transcendent character of the experience he attempts to describe.

The affair comes to a dramatic ending that precipitates the crisis of the novel. The lovers find tragedy through a mutual failure of trust, although ironically the lack of faith is primarily Yarrow's. Unable to shake off the puritanical doctrine of the Sturch, which proscribes alcohol and tobacco (as fundamentalist groups do today), Yarrow agonizes over Jeannette's moderate drinking, and substitutes a synthetic liquid, Easyglow, for the alcohol.

Jeannette becomes pregnant and dies in childbirth, the alcohol in reality being a contraceptive for her species, as Yarrow learns too late from Fobo, his Ozagenian mentor. Fobo explains that the lalitha are a parasitic female species of arthropod ancestry. They are able to reproduce with the aid of a human male, although conception occurs by means of the mouth, through salivary ova within the lalitha which are fertilized when an orgasm occurs.

Thanks to their peculiar biology, the lalitha have enjoyed a distinguished history, according to Fobo. They have become specialists in the art of love, which they have been able to perfect during their millenary lifespans. Only childbirth causes their deaths. In some cultures they have been worshipped as goddesses. "Religions were established in which the lalitha were the immortal goddess, and the ephemeral kings and priests were their lovers," Fobo informs Yarrow. By being perfect mistresses, the lalitha gained power, but earned the hatred of cultures which sought to exterminate them. "In the lalitha nature wrought the complete female," Fobo sums up, seeing the female primarily as a lover, rather than as a mother or person of intellect—an unsatisfactory view which may nevertheless represent the author's opinion at this point in his career.

Not only does Yarrow lose his archetypal sex goddess, but in his grief he comes into ironic conflict with the officials of the Sturch. A sinister officer named Macneff—whose name might suggest Joseph McCarthy—describes Yarrow's affair as disgusting, and urges him to repudiate it, threatening retaliatory punishment. In a final irony, Yarrow is saved by the supposedly harmless Ozagenians, who shrewdly suspect the earthmen of treachery, and blow up their ship before the terrestrials can bring nuclear destruction to Ozagen. But though given his life and freedom, Yarrow is broken by the tragedy of Jeannette; underscoring its irony, the novel ends with his bitter cry, "Jeannette? Jeannette? If only you had loved me enough to tell me...."

The Lovers aims for romantic tragedy, but it does not quite succeed in avoiding a melodramatic tone. The satirical vision of the novel is more successful than the romantic drama. This is not to say that the latter lacks strength. But Yarrow, for all his intelligence, is often an exasperating hero, clever and obtuse by turns, strangely lacking in curiosity about Jeannette. His final despairing words are doubly ironic, since it was his lack of trust that brought on Jeannette's death. Moreover, the reader wonders whether Yarrow, with his puritanical attitudes, could have accepted the truth. Still, the hero's weaknesses make him more effective as a character. Further, Yarrow's distrust of his lover, his inability to accept the feminine principle completely, is one of the costs exacted by his puritanism, and one of the important themes of the novel.

Farmer's novel must be read on the level of myth to be fully appreciated. Jeannette, for example, is not entirely credible as a character on the level of conventional realism. She is more successful when considered as a dream image or a romantic archetype of the daimonic woman. The name "lalitha" indicates that we are dealing with a rationalized version of the Lilith archetype, the seductive temptress whom Hebraic mythology opposed to the sedate, wifely figure of Eve. Lilith avatars occur frequently in Romantic fiction, sometimes playing a beneficent role, but more frequently assuming an ambiguous or sinister character: George MacDonald's nineteenth century romance, *Lilith*, is a classic rendition of the latter situation.

In Farmer's romance, Jeannette plays an affirmative role, initiating the hero into sexual experience his society forbids. She only becomes an ambiguous figure, taking on the character of the daimonic woman who abandons her mate, when her lover loses faith in her and meddles with the relationship. Although tragic, the experience has not been sterile, because Yarrow, the lover, is left with his memories and the daughters to whom Jeannette gave birth as symbols of fulfilled love.

When we turn from the symbolism of *The Lovers* to the larger themes of the novel, we see that Farmer satirizes his bigoted, rationalistic dystopia by making it a sterile, masculine world that has rejected the feminine principle. Consequently, its men, even an intelligent and sensitive one like Yarrow, are incomplete as human beings. Although Yarrow seeks and finds a sense of wholeness or unity by embracing the feminine principle in Jeannette—C. G. Jung, the psychoanalytic theorist, would call her the *anima*—he is unable to liberate himself from his father-dominated conditioning, and falters in his rebellious love. Yarrow's awareness is enlarged by his tragic experience, but he has yet to become a complete man, in Farmer's terms, at the end of the novel. Thus, *The Lovers* not only satirizes religious bigotry and technological sterility while celebrating sexuality; it also proposes on a subtler level the problem of masculine acceptance of the feminine principle in order to achieve psychic wholeness. This is a problem that future Farmer protagonists will often struggle against.

A final assessment of *The Lovers* is difficult to make, because the novel, though fairly mature in style, is uneven on the level of characterization and action, while simultaneously arousing dense and rich mythic resonances. *The Lovers* is a work of inventiveness and originality of vision, and it shows Farmer's ability to reach the deeper places in the unconscious through the invoking of archetypal symbols. First as a story, then as a novel, it has proved durable for nearly three decades. It is the most important of the works Farmer published in the fifties and early sixties, and it is likely to be considered an important American science fiction novel for quite a while.

Unfortunately, a companion novel to *The Lovers*, absurdly titled *A Woman a Day* (story version 1953; novel version 1960; also called *Timestop* by Lancer in 1968), deserves no such praise. This sequel is a sensationalized melodrama set on the Earth of the Sturch, describing the overthrow of its dystopian society, mainly through the exertions of Dr. Leif Barker and his friends. Barker is a cardboard superhero in the worst pulp tradition, often acting with a macho style unusual in the early Farmer; his attitudes toward women display a male chauvinism not present in any other Farmer hero. The incidents and characters of this novel are, largely forgettable. Undoubtedly, there was the possibility of a good novel in the downfall of the Sturch, but Farmer does not come close to realizing the potential of the theme in this pulpy narrative. *A Woman a Day* possess the faults of much magazine science fiction: sketchy characterizations and melodramatic action at the expense of credibility. However, its satire on the Sturch is consistent with that of *The Lovers*; both novels are essentially fifties' protests against the dominant cultural tone of America. Whatever its faults, *A Woman* eased the way for Farmer's composition of the novel-length version of *The Lovers*.

(2)

Aside from *The Lovers*, Farmer was more fortunate and successful as a short story writer than a novelist in his first dozen years as a professional (1952-63). As we have noted, the original Riverworld novel remained unpublished during these years, and *A Woman a Day* is an inferior work. *The Green Odyssey* (1957), Farmer's first published novel, is a readable but conventional adventure story discussed briefly elsewhere. *Fire and the Night* (1962) is a mainstream novel dealing with an interracial love affair. Like much of Farmer's work, it was ahead of its time and did not achieve commercial success. In shorter forms, however, Farmer's work was more accomplished and commercially successful, although even here Farmer sometimes had difficulty placing stories in science fiction magazines because their themes were considered too radical.

The early short fiction generally assails stereotypes, myths of religion and sex, and complacent notions of historical progress. "The First Robot," rejected by various editors and eventually lost by Farmer portrayed women as having been used as tools or robots from the time of the cave men. The relationship between human and alien lovers reappears in another important and controversial story from this period, "My Sister's Brother." (Indeed, Farmer became so identified with the erotic bond between human and alien that his first volume of short stories, in which "My Sister's Brother" was reprinted, was called *Strange Relations*.) "My Sister's Brother" shows some similarities to *The Lovers*: again there is a naive and repressed hero, a victim of puritanical religious conditioning. Again there is a lovely alien woman, Martia, whom the hero meets on Mars, where both are explorers. Martia differs from human females, however, by lacking conventional genitalia below the waist. Lane is attracted to Martia, but instead of starting an affair, he subliminates his desires into feelings of brotherhood between human and alien. When Lane learns the way Martia's species reproduces, however, he finds her repulsive and the story moves to an ironic denouement.

Martia carries a "larva" or wormlike embryo in her throat engendered by two others of her race, the Eeltua. This larva is both a potential child, and a phallus that will fertilize her ova, but only when she is excited by expressions

15

of affection from another adult. So complex a system of reproduction reduces the human conception of parentage and ancestry to absurdity. This biological arrangement is also esthetically disgusting to Lane, who imagines that all humans will share his feelings of nausea. (As in *The Lovers*, the alien woman's reproductive system operates partly by means of oral sexual responses; as Leslie Fiedler remarks, oral sexuality is a repetitive theme in Farmer's work.)

"My Sister's Brother" ends ironically when Lane destroys the larva or fetus of his alien companion, and is only prevented from killing Martia herself by the fortuitous arrival of some of her Eeltuan companions. Instead of punishing Lane, the Eeltua treat Lane compassionately, considering him a victim of rigid conditioning. Even Martia, heartbroken by the loss of her fetus, hopes that Lane will outgrow his ethnocentrism under enlightened teaching. Less rebellious than Yarrow in *The Lovers*, Farmer's protagonist is, despite some feelings of compassion, an ethnocentric and puritanical bigot, unable to accept what seems to him the strange, "unnatural" biology of the alien female. On a symbolic level, the story again emphasizes that the male who reacts with fear and revulsion to the feminine principle, even when embodied in a being who offends his sense of order, can never be psychically whole.

Interestingly enough, "My Sister's Brother" seems to have encountered more resistance than most of Farmer's early work. In a note in *The Book of Philip Jose Farmer*, Farmer describes its rejection by John W. Campbell at *Astounding*. Farmer was convinced by this refusal that Horace Gold at *Galaxy*, sometimes more liberal than Campbell, would also reject the story. It was eventually published in *Fantasy and Science Fiction*, but only after first being rejected by Robert Mills, and then purchased by another editor for a magazine that never appeared. To his credit, Mills then had a change of heart and bought the story, which was finally published in 1960. The history of this story shows that, although Farmer had chosen a genre supposedly open to innovation and challenging ideas, he sometimes had to contend with the resistance of editors, especially in the fifties when they may have been more cautious about their readers' reactions than they needed to be.

Another fifties story later reprinted in *Strange Relations*, "Mother" (1953), depicts ironically the passive surrender of a mother-dominated young man to an alien maternal creature who literally swallows him. Eddie Fetts, an effeminate opera star, has been overly dependent on his mother, a strong-minded scientist. Eddie's marriage is also a failure, reinforcing his inability to achieve a manly sense of independence. When mother and son are shipwrecked on a strange planet, Eddie relies on his mother for survival. But Eddie is swallowed by a gigantic immobile maternal being, becoming a living parasite inside this creature, in the womb where she also nurses her young. Anything mobile is generically male to this female monster, who absorbs moving animals to irritate a sensitive area of her womb, an action producing conception. For a time Eddie hopes that his human mother will rescue him, but she is eventually destroyed by his host, and Eddie settles down to a comfortably passive existence, forgetting that he ever enjoyed the outer world.

Though on the literal level the biology of the maternal monster is carefully depicted, this story must clearly be read as psychological allegory. The tale seems to describe neurotic dependence on a mother figure, becoming a psychotic surrender to a devouring maternal archetype, symbolized by literal residence in the womb. Here the feminine principle is depicted as a voracious monster when not counterbalanced by a strong masculine figure. This vision of a frightening mother figure is quite unusual in Farmer's work, however, and the importance of the story in Farmer's canon is somewhat exaggerated by Fiedler.

Still another 1950s story (also reprinted in *Strange Relations*), "Father" (1955) satirizes the Judaic and Christian concept of a father god ruling over a static creation. This story also marks an early but forceful appearance by Farmer's wandering priest, John Carmody, who figures in many Farmer stories, both as a voice of discriminating judgment and as something of a comic trickster.

The "father" in this story is a strange and powerful giant ruling an Edenic planet as a benevolent despot and demigod. The father, although his nature and power are natural rather than supernatural, watches over his world like the God of Genesis: he heals his creatures as though he is divine, and possesses the ability to restore them to life when they die. Discovered by an expedition from Earth of which Carmody is a member, this Edenic planet possesses theological and moral problems akin to the Lithia in James Blish's *A Case of Conscience* (perhaps an influence, for a novelette version of this had appeared in 1953). Carmody, after studying the rule of "Father," decides that the apparent benevolence is oppressive, preventing his creatures from developing independence. Moreover, the animals on the planet Abatos have become fat and complacent, since the evolutionary struggle for existence no longer hones their skills; with death followed by an automatic resurrection, the animals no longer have to pay the full price of failure in the struggle for existence.

Father's disapproval of sexual intercourse has prompted him to eliminate all male animals from his Eden. Yet his pleasure in resurrecting the animals is described as a kind of surrogate sexual experience by Carmody. Carmody denounces Father's dominance as egotism, a demonic parody of the Christian concept of an overruling providence; and he condemns Father's world as a false paradise, a sterile and static Eden ruled by a megalomaniac. Conflict develops when Carmody's religious superior, a more susceptible man, disagrees with Carmody. Bishop Andre, a gentle and saintly man, regards the paternal ruler as an image of God's divine benevolence, and contemplates taking over Father's role when the latter proposes to travel across the galaxy. The bishop is a man excessively subservient to a dominating human father, and hence inclined to conceive of God as a tyrannical and cruel figure.

Carmody's opinion of Father is confirmed by the story's action. The priest witnesses an obscene ritual in which Father orders his beasts to destroy him, and then afterward resurrects himself. Carmody condemns Father and his pretensions to deity, commenting that "in his vast egoism, he resembles the old pagan deities of Earth, who were supposed to have slain themselves and then, having made the supreme sacrifice, resurrected themselves. " Although Carmody restricts his comparison to pagan gods, the reader may conclude that Farmer's satire goes further, to include the Christian concept of Christ's death and resurrection.

Even Carmody's bishop comes around to Carmody's opinion. Rather than take the giant's place on Abatos, the bishop commits suicide, thus violating the ethics of his church, because he fears that Father's taking the gift of resurrection to the galaxy will produce an idolatrous worship of Father. Carmody will not allow the bishop to be resurrected, but he does give him a Christian burial. Carmody considers the bishop's suicide an act of conscience. As the spaceship leaves Abatos and Father, Carmody pronounces this judgment: "He was no god. *He* was the Father . . . of lies."

Whatever one thinks of the artistry of this story, "Father" is clearly an imaginative satire on an image of divinity that Farmer sees as childish and sterile. Insofar as established religions like Judaism and Christianity foster and sustain an image of God as a solitary puritannical creator who condemns sex and is opposed to change, Farmer sees them as guilty of perpetuating an inadequate and harmful myth. However, Farmer does not completely reject religious images of God, for he makes Carmody the spokesman for a more humane concept of a creator than the one satirized in the story:

> Aren't we in one sense the focus of creation, the Creator's image? Surely He too likes to feel a need for relief and finds it in laughter. Perhaps His laughter does not come out as mere meaningless noise but is manifested on a more highly economical and informative level. Perhaps He tosses off a new galaxy, instead of having a belly-laugh. Or substitutes a chuckle with a prodding of a species up the Jacob's ladder of evolution toward a more human state.

The religious satire in "Father" is ultimately premised on the absurdity, according to Farmer's vision, of the masculine principle trying to dominate existence or to live without a creative relationship with the feminine. This theme, of course, suggests a further theological application: religions with an excessively masculine conception or image of God are necessarily unsatisfactory without an enlargement of their mythology to include a counterbalancing image of the feminine principle.

Another early story worth discussion is "Sail On! Sail On!" (1952). Less concerned with religion and sex than the tales discussed above, this playful narrative constructs an alternate world, revealing in the process Farmer's flexibility of mind and technical craftsmanship. "Sail On! Sail On!" is a neat *tour de force* describing in a few thousand words a credible world where Roger Bacon was not persecuted by the church, but founded an advanced science with ecclesiastical support. Set in the radio operator's room of one of Columbus's ships, the tale moves to a final comic revelation, just as the reader believes that he understands all of Farmer's alterations of history: the earth in this universe is flat, and Columbus's ships sail off the edge.

The construction of worlds in alternate historical timestreams is one of science fiction's most imaginative uses of history; such stories, although they may often be trivial exercises, display the ability of science fiction to explore the imaginative potential of numerous extrapolations from known history. Although "Sail On! Sail On!" is a relatively lightweight work, it gently mocks our notions of historical progress and gives early evidence of the liberal and speculative qualities of Farmer's mind.

Perhaps the most memorable of Farmer's short stories from his first period is "The Alley Man," which ran second in the voting for the Hugo Awards of 1960, losing to Daniel Keyes' "Flowers for Algernon," which later provided the basis for the successful film, *Charly*. Closer to conventional realism than usual for Farmer, "The Alley Man" portrays the last days of a lusty, one-armed ragpicker, who lives in a shanty on a city dump near Kickapoo Creek, outside the central Illinois city of Onaback (a thinly disguised Peoria). For the story, Farmer draws on his experience of working in a steel mill in

Bartonville, a community neighboring the no man's land where Paley resides.

The "Alley Man," or Old Man Paley, is a Rabelaisian drinker and wencher, a misfit in twentieth-century technological America. Living in magnificent squalor with two slatternly mistresses, he is said to have fathered a number of bastards. More at home in alleys than on main streets or in houses, he ekes out a living by scavenging through the trash cans on the "west bluff," one of the town's older, more respectable areas (based on an existing Peoria neighborhood of that name). Paley is enough of a local phenomenon to have been brought in for observation by psychiatrists at a hospital for the mentally ill, where he proved impervious to conventional psychological examinations. Considered something of an enigma, Paley is observed during the narrative by a graduate student in anthropology doing research on an advanced degree.

Dorothy Singer, the graduate student, is both fascinated and repelled by Paley, yet she finds his lifestyle a refreshing contrast to bourgeois respectability. Her involvement with Paley ultimately destroys him. She is intrigued by the personal myth Paley has constructed (or perhaps inherited) to justify his individualism. Paley claims to be the last true descendant of the paleolithic or neanderthal men (hence the name "Paley") who dominated the world fifty thousand years ago, before the appearance of homo sapiens. According to a legend supposedly passed on by Paley's ancestors, the paleolithic men lost their final battle with the usurping race when a traitorous woman stole their chieftain's totem, a hat. Whereas the new breed of humans worshiped a mother goddess and founded a matriarchy (here Farmer follows the speculations of Robert Graves and some anthropologists), the neanderthals, a virile patriarchy, worshiped the "Old Guy in the Sky," a pagan sky god to whom Paley still renders a rather defiant and unchristianized worship. Paley attributes the generations of his people's subservience to homo sapiens as resulting from the loss of their totem object and the defeat of their religion by the matriarchal creed.

The identification of Paley with the neanderthal myth gives the story a science fiction angle, although the truth or falsity of Paley's claims is allowed to remain ambiguous. Here Farmer shows artistic tact, for the tale gains esthetic strength from the ambiguity of myth. Dorothy finds the story sufficiently credible to mention it to her professor of anthropology, but the latter treats it with the usual scepticism of respected scientific authority. Deena, one of Paley's mistresses, insists that Paley constructed the myth from reading comic books, an opinion that seems plausible.

The story's crisis is precipitated by Dorothy when she makes a replica of the long lost magic hat and gives it to Paley. Paley reveals a tender side by taking Dorothy to a secret copse or grove on the tree-covered west bluff, his personal sacred place, and seducing her there. Paley considers Dorothy a special lover, not one of his ordinary fornications, but Dorothy, suddenly growing aware of how much society would disapprove of her, is appalled at herself. Ironically, when she comes to Paley's shack in a driving rainstorm to end the affair, Paley's jealous mistress kills Paley in the pelting rain near a flooding Kickapoo Creek.

As bizarre and coarse as Paley's life is, the character is portrayed vigorously, and he wins our grudging sympathy by his spirit of heroic defiance. His crude worship of the "Old Guy in the Sky" gives Paley a kind of tragic dignity, and the tragic irony of his death elicits sympathy. In "The Alley Man" Farmer has created a small tragic drama out of homely materials.

Moreover, "The Alley Man" shows Farmer's fascination with primitive vitality, and his concern to create sympathetic and often heroic figures whose strength is drawn from sources outside industrial civilization. The tale counterpoints Farmer's use of matriarchal fertility myth in *The Lovers*, although Paley sees himself and his people as victims of that myth. Clearly however, Paley is a tarnished image of the noble savage debased and finally destroyed by industrial civilization. The story also points forward to Farmer's later novels that seek to exploit remaining sources of primitive strength—especially the books dealing with the Tarzan myth and the "World of Tiers" series, where the heroes are identified with the potent warrior tradition of the American Indian.

Although *The Lovers* and such stories as "The Alley Man" seem to strike a dominant tone of bitter romantic rebellion in Farmer's work through 1962, Farmer also published some work of a more humorous and relaxed spirit during this time. Our treatment of this period has been necessarily selective, but it has not distorted the picture. At this time Farmer was more accomplished in the short story or novelette form than the novel, although the book-length version of *The Lovers*, and to some extent, *The Green Odyssey*, do show a growing competence in the novel. Undoubtedly, of course, our view of Farmer's first period would be clearer if the original Riverworld novel had been published by Shasta, or even if the manuscript of this book were published intact at this late date (a possibility which Farmer has considered). But clearly his early period shows Farmer attacking current dogma and social attitudes by vigorous satire, while endowing neglected myths with new imaginative power.

II
The Speculative Iconoclast

(1)

Farmer's iconoclastic spirit and his determination to assault sexual and religious dogmas is evident in many of the novels he published in the middle and late sixties, during the second part of his career. Humor and satire are more prominent in these works, although Farmer never allows a particular tone to dominate. In fact, there is great contrast between the individual novels, from the romantic intensity of *Night of Light* (1966) to the jocular spirit of *Flesh* (first published in 1960, revised in 1968). Moreover, Farmer continued to be speculative and exploratory, with the same bold spirit of his fifties work (indeed, some of the novels are expansions of 1950s short stories and novelettes). At this same time, however, Farmer also began writing a number of entertaining adventure novels for Ace Books, obviously with a more commercial market in mind. These books helped Farmer develop his professional skills as a novelist, and will be examined separately in a later part of this critique.

(2)

A caustic satire, *Inside Outside* (1964) carries on the dystopian spirit of *The Lovers*, but also speculates about the ironies or perhaps the ultimate absurdity of human existence, with some interesting foreshadowings of the Riverworld saga. Unfortunately, Farmer leads us over a somewhat bumpy narrative, with too many themes, and passages of flat writing which may have resulted from the author's having hurried to his conclusion.

Inside Outside is an arid desert world inside a sphere, an environment about which Farmer's anti-hero, Jack Cull (suggesting "jackal") speculates in the opening passages, wondering whether he is actually living in a literal hell. Trapped in a society of strict hierarchal levels, like the executive structure of a large corporation, Cull struggles to hold his own in a world devoted to the pursuit of social status, power, and hedonistic sex. Although Farmer is usually sympathetic toward liberal sexual behavior, sex in this society is merely a commodity. Cull himself, a cynical lackey of the establishment, has a loveless relationship with a social climber, a career woman named Phyllis Nystrom.

The dystopia depicted in the first third of this novel makes satirical thrusts at the corporation-dominated, credit card- and consumer-oriented society of America of the early 1960s. Not only does Farmer satirize the sexual attitudes and social mores of our world, but he also mocks organized religion, with synthetic Christs—actually androids—being hawked like used cars by an evangelist who seems a caricature of Dostoevsky. Adding to this bizarre atmosphere are enigmatic creatures shaped like the demons in illustrated editions of Dante.

One-third of the way into his book, Farmer abruptly veers in an unexpected direction. The world inside the sphere is upset by a cataclysm, so that some of the characters inside it are literally thrown "outside." Farmer's heroes and heroines usually grow morally only when they are forced to confront their own survival, and Cull and Nystrom become a little more likable when they find themselves fighting for their lives. However, the anti-hero and -heroine of this tale are woefully unsympathetic from the first, and only gradually gain stature as the story progresses (even then, the heroine matures very little). By the end of the novel, Cull has become a compassionate humanist, and the reader has fallen asleep.

In its final sections the novel turns from the struggle for survival to some possible explanations for the artificial universe the characters inhabit. In a long expository dialogue with a figure called X (another anticipation of Riverworld), Cull is given some unpleasant answers. Farmer draws on the ancient myth of "pre-existence," but rationalizes it with naturalist postulates. Cull and his fellow inhabitants of the "inside" world of the sphere are indeed victims of powerful manipulators—not gods or demons, but an intelligent race called "The Immortals," who, despite their calculated management of others, are supposedly benevolent. Although these "Immortals" have invented an artificial "soul" that will ensure life after death, the world of the novel is revealed to be a realm of pre-existent souls where ethical standards are programmed into humans before birth. The "Immortals" have not been very successful with their moral programming: the "pre-existence" experience is said to engender conflicts which nullify much of the ethical training. Moreover, Farmer's characters will forget their pre-existent life after birth, and be separated from each other (a condition that makes their lives before birth even more insignificant). Farmer achieves a surprising and ironic ending here, but his philosophical speculation raises more questions than it answers.

In short, *Inside Outside* has a dual purpose: it attempts not only to present a dystopian satire, but to offer a metaphysical statement about human life at the mercy of mysterious and godlike forces. Moreover, the novel raises the question whether life is meaningless apart from the wisdom and compassion humans bring to it. When Farmer explores the inadequacy of rational efforts to give life meaning, he still does not succeed in convincing us imaginatively that life is absurd. His hero's meditations at the novel's end stress the need for compassion for humanity, and we remain convinced that the ethical behavior that the immortals are trying to inculcate is worthwhile. Whatever his reason tells us, Farmer's imagination usually resists the conclusion that life is worthless.

A final judgment on the novel is difficult. Although the satire is lively and the catastrophe seems impressive, the philosophical speculations at the end are disappointing. The novel seems to suffer from its divided aims: a social satire may sometimes be used as a vehicle for metaphysical quest, but the purposes are awkwardly combined here. The book is also marred by a prevailing bitterness of tone unusual in Farmer's work. For all its energy, it seems, unfortunately, an ambitious failure.

(3)

The novel *Dare* (1965; adapted from a 1953 magazine serial) is one of several Farmer novels published in the sixties with roots in his earlier period. Here again Farmer satirizes sexual puritanism and an excessively masculine world view by returning to his old theme of love between human and alien. A more conventional initiation story than *The Lovers*, *Dare* has a formulaic happy ending, but its characterizations are more assured. While less intellectually ambitious than *Inside Outside*, *Dare* is better constructed and less strident in the presentation of its theme.

The setting illustrates Farmer's formidable talents for extrapolation and the construction of an imaginary world. Dare is a planet peopled by transplanted humans, the descendants of the lost Roanoke colony established by Sir Walter Raleigh. (The name Dare derives from Virginia Dare.) Farmer's premise is that the Roanoke colonists were transported across space to a planet in the Tau Ceti system. Their society is an agrarian world of primitive technology, dominated by patriarchal Elizabethan attitudes, blended with religious puritanism and racism. It is a detailed and convincing construct.

The conflict in the novel derives from the fact that the humans must share the planet with an alien species. The Horstels are a humanoid race, their main physical difference being long hairy tails resembling those of horses (hence their name, from "horsetails"). Psychologically, the Horstels are emotional and intuitive, closer to the earth and to primitive sources of wisdom than humans. Since the Horstels are peaceful and more sensible than the transplanted terrestrials, it is not surprising that the humans have developed a plan to exterminate them with a treacherous attack.

Farmer's hero, Jack Cage, is another of Farmer's naive young men of good will, although he proves to be somewhat more adaptable than Hal Yarrow. Sympathetic to the Horstels, Cage falls in love with R'li, a Horstel maiden, who is witty, nubile, charming, and one of Farmer's most attractive heroines. After some initial resistance, Cage becomes R'li's lover, and rebels against his society's racist and patriarchial anti-feminine attitudes. Transcending human ethnocentrism, he accepts the Horstel point of view, with its less rational and more intuitive approach to experience. Eventually, after various complications, Cage and R'li defeat the human genocide plan, and work to develop a new understanding between the races. Although Cage has revolted both against his father and tradition, he emerges as a responsible social leader at the end of the novel.

Dare is the story of a young man's erotic and moral initiation; it is a satisfying depiction, despite elements of melodrama, of the passage from youth to manhood. As usual, manhood and wholeness in Farmer's fiction is achieved by an acceptance of the feminine principle, or what C. G. Jung called the *anima*. The *anima* often appears initially to a naive male in an alien and somewhat ambiguous form. Unlike some of Farmer's early protagonists, Cage successfully manages to make the transition to a more enlightened philosophy.

It should be noted that *Dare* comes much closer to an explicit criticism of white racism than much of Farmer's other writing in the fifties and sixties. The middle 1960s, when the novel was published, were a time when racial tensions in America were being expressed in ways that would eventually alter American society; at this crucial moment, *Dare* makes a fairly obvious comment on the need for understanding and equality.

(4)

More ambitious than *Dare*, *Night of Light* (1966; expanded from a 1957 Carmody story) tackles more directly the religious themes expressed in the earlier novels. This well-crafted story is presented in two parts: the first describes John Carmody's religious conversion; the second deals with the transformation of a mother goddess religion from a local planetary cult to a more universal faith, as the change is witnessed twenty-seven years later by Father John Carmody, now a Roman Catholic priest of the Order of St. Jairus. A central figure in the novel, though she never appears, is the mother goddess, Boonta, the focus of worship on Dante's Joy. Although earlier Farmer works had commented on the need for recognition of the feminine principle, and *The Lovers* had mentioned the "Great Mother" (the mythic incarnation of the feminine principle of Robert Graves' *The White Goddess*), this is the first time that Farmer uses a mother goddess endowed with numinous or sacred awe and supernatural powers.

The society of Kareem, or Dante's Joy, worships the goddess Boonta, who rules through her mortal consort and son, the incarnation of the god Yess. Yess is a moral but forgiving god, somewhat like Jesus, associated with light and moral perfection; but he is occasionally challenged by the goddess's other son, his darker brother Algul. This happens at the primary holy period of Boontism, a seven-day festival (or ordeal) once every seven years called the "Night of Light." A time of epiphany and the changing of the gods, the Night of Light allows Algul to battle Yess, but usually Algul loses. By some peculiar transformation, those worshippers who stay awake during the Night experience psychic epiphanies; that is, unconscious anxieties and fantasies are projected in material embodiments. During the festival the law is suspended and there are many fatalities; those who survive may have new identities, or be purged of inner resistance to their religious beliefs. Most worshippers, however, avoid the Night by staying indoors and taking a drug that renders them impervious to its influence. Whether the mystical events of the Night of Light are supernatural is left ambiguous in this novel, an unusual practice for Farmer, but one that is esthetically satisfying here.

In Part One of the novel, the story of Carmody's conversion is presented through events that demonstrate the psychology of conversion. When Carmody arrives on Dante's Joy, he is known throughout the galaxy as a professional assassin and thief, guilty of the reprehensible crime of murdering his wife and unborn child. Since Carmody considers the universe meaningless and human life a joke, he justifies his amoral outlook as the only sensible response to such an existence. In the context of Farmer's vision, Carmody's besetting fault is his excessively masculine outlook: he believes himself hard, shrewd, pragmatic, independent of the need for others. Carmody's murder of his wife and unborn child means, symbolically, that he has tried to destroy the feminine side of his psyche, and with it his potential for innocence. As is clear by now, any Farmer character who rejects the feminine principle is tragically incomplete and fated to suffer.

Despite his rationalizations, Carmody cannot evade his guilt, although he tries to repress it with further crimes. The image of his murdered wife appears to Carmody on the "Night of Light" in several forms as the action unfolds in a series of surrealistic scenes. After trying to kill his "wife" again and again to deny his guilt, Carmody conceives the idea of the ultimate crime: he will break into the temple of Boonta and murder the man who represents the incarnation of the god Yess. Afterward, trapped beside the statue of the mother goddess by worshippers of both Yess and Algul, Carmody again confronts the projection of his wife, a very maternal figure. Surrendering to his guilt, he chooses to make her unborn child the new incarnation of Yess, the god of moral goodness. This symbolic acceptance of his wife and child, and his choice of good, are the signs of Carmody's conversion from an amoral self to a moral personality which acknowledges responsibility for past crimes. Thus John Carmody the assassin will, after a period of discipline and mortification, become Father John Carmody the priest.

Farmer's study of Carmody's conversion reveals a sound knowledge of religious psychology, and is depicted in a series of effective scenes with hallucinatory images. The "Night of Light" is a period when the contents of the unconscious are brought into consciousness and acknowledged; Carmody's recognition of his guilt and acceptance of his *anima* brings about a restructuring of his personality.

By contrast with Carmody's psychic drama, Part Two of *Night of Light* is less intense and flawed by unnecessary melodrama. Carmody, now the enlightened Christian humanist of the other Carmody stories, returns to Dante's Joy on a mission twenty-seven years after his conversion. Carmody had suffered a breakdown after leaving Dante's Joy, following his traumatic experiences on the Night of Light; a mystical experience in Johns Hopkins Hospital had convinced Carmody to become a priest. The established religions, however, are losing converts all over the universe to Boontism, now no longer a local cult but a proselytizing faith with universal pretensions. His superiors send Carmody to Dante's Joy to report on Boontism, and the Boontists welcome Carmody, since he is one of the seven mystic fathers of the reigning incarnation of Yess—and, of course, the biological father of the god.

A new stage in Boontism is about to evolve. Yess, acting on behalf of his mother goddess, has decreed that all worshippers must undergo the psychic trial of the Night of Light, an ordeal that only the strong will survive. A meeting with his son, Yess, convinces Carmody that Yess is indeed acting under some powerful unconscious influence, presumably the dictates of the goddess. Yess has even written, under divine possession, a book about Boontism, the last chapter being a prediction of the outcome of this year's Night of Light. At the festival the followers of Yess are driven by violence from the temple by the followers of Algul, his darker brother. When a baby is born as the new incarnation of Algul, Yess and his followers go into temporary exile. But a reconciliation and a new order are promised. Such a new order seems to be an attempt by the goddess to bring Yess and Algul together in a synthesis which will enlarge the appeal of Boontism to embrace both the light and the dark, in a vision of wholeness representing a further stage in the evolution of the faith.

Even Carmody, the witness to these events, leaves Dante's Joy with his own faith shaken. He wonders if he too might be an instrument of the goddess, destined as an observer to testify to the power of Boontism and contribute to the decline of Catholicism. However, the novel affirms the reality and significance of religious experience, whatever form it takes.

Night of Light is one of Farmer's most successful novels. It is Farmer's testimony to the power of religious myth. Religious myth for Farmer is a basic need of the mind, but one which takes varying mutations. *Night of Light* suggests that an outworn mythology of the father god may be replaced in the future by the mythology of a mother goddess, an embodiment of the feminine principle. Although Boontism is by no means a perfect religion, Farmer endows it with an imaginative power which he cannot give to a religion like Christianity, with its mythology of a divine father. Farmer does pay a kind of homage to Christianity by creating the figure of John Carmody as a spokesman for an enlightened and compassionate humanism. But it is not until much later in his career, with *Jesus on Mars*, that Farmer recreates Christian myth with a sense of numinous power, and even then only when he describes the divine son, Jesus. Clearly *Night of Light* shows Farmer's vision as centered on the transcendence of the feminine principle.

(5)

Despite *Night of Light*, Farmer does not see the return of a matriarchal religion as the solution to human conflict or the way back to a lost paradise. What would an earth dominated by the religion of the Great Mother be like? Farmer speculates on the answer to this question in *Flesh* (1968, a revision of a 1960 version).

This picture of a future civilization dominated by a matriarchal religion is quite different from the romantic utopia envisioned in Robert Graves' *Watch the Northwind Rise*, although it shares a few features of Graves' fictional society. But where Graves' novel was essentially solemn, Farmer finds such a future world almost indescribably amusing. *Flesh* is in fact Farmer's most thoroughly sustained comic novel of the first two decades of his career. There are elements of comedy in earlier Farmer novels, notably in *The Green Odyssey*, but nowhere before does Farmer so completely show his talent for ribald humor. The result is like a Restoration comedy or a Fielding novel as rewritten by Jack London, and set in an America 900 years in the future.

Farmer's plot concerns a space expedition that returns to America in 2860 after eight hundred years in suspended animation. The astronauts find a post-industrial world split up into small agrarian countries, and devoted to the worship of a Great Mother, called, appropriately enough, Columbia. The goddess is feted in ritualized orgies, a reversal of our present and more austere forms of Christianity with their mythology of a father god.

Commander Peter Stagg, the leader of the expedition, suffers from a reversal of the usual problem of Farmer's naive heroes: whereas Hal Yarrow and other Farmer heroes struggle against sexual inhibition, Stagg is the victim of a sexual potency too great to be controlled. Stagg's extraordinary powers are artificially induced by the priests of Columbia, who graft to his head antlers containing an aphrodisiac. Stagg thus becomes the Horned King of Celtic legend, a consort of the goddess who is expected to satisfy her female votaries at communal orgies.

Although Stagg's situation would seem the realization of most men's fantasies, his lack of control renders him a comic figure. Moreover, he complains, his performances for the goddess occur while he is in a trance which does not allow personal awareness or enjoyment. In fact, he comes to dread the oncoming orgies as an exhausting ordeal. Quantity definitely does not equal quality. As the Sunhero (also a pun on "son-hero"), Stagg's situation is both unenviable and ridiculous.

After many comic adventures, during which Stagg and his fellows journey from one wacky principality to another in the new America, Stagg finally sees a remedy for his unhappiness in the removal of his horns, and in his marriage to Mary Casey, a virgin raised according to the old Catholic faith. The novel ends with Stagg extricated from his predicament, and his capacity to love normally restored by his marriage. The novel thus suggests that sexual excess may be an unnatural state (at least for ordinary man), for which the cure is the form of chastity called married love. Moderation becomes a sensible alternative to the fantasies of erotic paradise.

The America of *Flesh* is hardly an earthly paradise, but it is a life-affirming world at the other extreme from the sterile dystopia of the Sturch. In a world where the feminine principle is elevated to divinity, there may be an overemphasis on fertility, but life itself is at least a healthy comedy rather than servitude under a dehumanizing tyranny.

Flesh is an uneven novel, rich in comic invention, but not always able to sustain the exuberance of its opening scenes. At times it resembles a trip through a penny arcade at the amusement park, but Farmer deserves special praise for one glorious touch of comic invention. His vision of baseball in the future depicts a game which has degenerated into a blood sport, with a lethal ball bulging with iron spikes. To bat successfully in such a game is to become a hero, or at least a survivor. Despite the brutality of the sport, the comic tone of the novel makes the deaths of unsuccessful batters seem insignificant. Farmer's genial spirit in *Flesh* is a sign of his growing mastery of materials and craft. Moreover, his ability to treat sexuality from a comic viewpoint anticipates the later development of his gifts for comedy.

(6)

It may have been Farmer's sense of humor as well as his desire to treat sexuality more explicitly that eventually led him to experiment with writing pornography. In the late sixties, Farmer agreed to write three books for Essex House, a firm that was marketing a line of sophisticated pornographic fiction beyond the level of juvenile sex fantasies.

Farmer has never shown any inclination to deny his authorship of *Image of The Beast*, *Blown*, and *A Feast Unknown*, viewing them as legitimate literary exercises in a particular form. Interestingly, Farmer remarks privately that he knew little about erotic fiction before writing these books; despite his omnivorous reading, he had encountered few of the underground "classics" of this genre. The ordinary plot of a pornographic romance, from *Fanny Hill* and de Sade to the twentieth century, is to take a naive virgin through a series of adventures in which she suffers a humiliating series of losses, both of dignity and chastity. This formula is repeated obsessively and fantastically. The ritual humiliations demean women; not surprisingly, most pornography is written by males for males, although occasionally a talented woman like Anais Nin will pander to masculine tastes. Many feminists regard such works as a sign of repulsive sexual stereotyping in our society. This pattern does not appear in Farmer's pornographic novels. Curiously, it is Farmer's men, rather than his women, who are the victims here. The author also adds a mixture of satire to remind the reader that he is merely playing a game.

Image of the Beast (1968), subtitled "an exorcism," is particularly amusing as a ribald parody of the Gothic novel. The anti-hero, one Herald Childe, is a bungling innocent who fancies himself a private detective (his name is, of course, a joking allusion to Byron's wandering pilgrim, Childe Harold). At times Childe's misadventures seem a comic parody of the serious sexual problems encountered by Farmer's earlier naive heroes. Childe roams a Los Angeles blighted by smog—a comic counterpart to the fogs and mists of traditional gothic fiction—and eventually investigates nefarious goings-on in an isolated mansion occupied by a sinister Count Igescu. Igescu, a vampire archetype, is actually an alien in disguise, for Farmer provides ingenious science fiction rationalizations for his gothic archetypes. In the gothic sexual world of the mansion Childe is a child indeed, being threatened and victimized by unspeakably bizarre sexual assaults, until rescued by the glamorous Dolores del Osorojo, supposedly a ghost from the days of Spanish California. Not only is Dolores no ghost, but she is an accomplished lover whose erotic skills have been perfected by centuries of experience.

Although *Image of the Beast* is primarily a burlesque of the gothic, Farmer at times is able to conjure up some genuine horrors. The description of a sex murder early in the novel is grisly enough to nauseate the police, not to mention the reader. Sexuality transmuted into violence is what is truly obscene and frightening, Farmer implies, not the papier-mache horrors of the popular gothic mode. This point of view is underscored by Farmer's caricature of the book collector, Woolston Heepish. Heepish is the ultimate fan, so obsessed with collecting movie posters and horror magazines that his mania wholly absorbs his life. His house is so cluttered that he hardly has room to open his refrigerator; yet he does not even understand the meaning of gothic archetypes. He is the consumate middle-aged child, a case of arrested adolescence flitting about with reckless delight in search of cardboard monsters. "Terror carried to the extreme became ordinary." Farmer says; Heepish's juvenile mania reduces horror to banality.

Although not as funny, *Blown* (1969), the sequel to *Image of the Beast*, continues Childe's pratfalls among the gothic aliens although this time Childe's escapades are counterpointed by the peregrinations of Forrest J Ackerman, a collector of gothic paraphernalia who replaces the Heepish of the earlier volume. Ackerman, an actual fan and well-known collector of science fiction books, is a friend of Farmer who enjoyed the Heepish caricature in the first volume. In *Blown* Ackerman scurries around on the fringe of the action, being lucky enough (or unlucky enough, depending on your point of view) to miss the novel's obligatory orgy.

On the whole, *Blown* is less lively than its predecessor, even though Farmer has added rain to the Los Angeles smog to increase the murkiness of the atmosphere (and to satirize Southern California's image as a paradise of sun and beaches). Childe has given up being a detective in this book, but he persists in snooping about and becoming a victim. Farmer achieves a scene of genuine horror when Childe, making love to a sinister woman named Vivienne Mabcrough, becomes the host of a male succubus who inhabits her body. On the whole, however, Farmer is more successful at parodying the classic gothic characters than at developing scenes of horror.

Farmer's descriptions of sex in the two volumes are fairly explicit, but they are on the whole emetic rather than prurient in their effect. The chief exorcism in the stories is the purgation (presumably in inhibited readers) of some uneasy feelings associated with varieties of unusual sexual activity. At times, however, the grotesque night world of Farmer's two novels creates by implication a respect for the wholeness and sanity of a world of more conventional sexuality.

As a sign that Farmer did not consider *Image of the Beast* and *Blown* a detour away from his other work, he wrote a third book to round out the trilogy. Published by Ballantine, *Traitor to the Living* (1973) is a novel of serious intrigue, quite conventional in its treatment of sex, and capable of being read independently of its predecessors. Beginning in Illinois, moving to the West Coast, and then returning, the story involves a quiet university professor, Gordon Carfax, on an investigation of a computer that supposedly allows contact with the dead. The novel still follows the gothic tradition, but with science fictional modifications. The machine with spiritualist powers, Medium, would probably be more at home in a Philip K. Dick novel, and the sinister aliens are a variation on a familiar type. Farmer achieves an unpleasant effect at one point when it is revealed, late in the story, that Carfax has been making love to his mistress after her body has been taken over by an alien. On the whole, however, *Traitor to the Living* not only lacks humor, but does not create much suspense either, proof again that Farmer is not especially stimulated by working in the gothic mode unless he approaches it in a spirit of parody.

(7)

If Farmer's first two experiments with the pornographic novel produced only lively parodies, the third effort is a more daring and important achievement. *A Feast Unknown* (1969) is Farmer's first fictional work to recreate the Tarzan mythology of Edgar Rice Burroughs, and as such, it is a pivotal work in Farmer's development. It manages to be an imaginative transformation of myth, while at the same time exploiting that myth for satire.

Farmer recreates two titanic pulp heroes, Tarzan and Doc Savage, and first puts them in combat with each other, then with the secret masters of the earth, the mysterious Nine. This is an outrageously pulpish plot that would have done honor to Edgar Rice Burroughs or Lester Dent (Kenneth Robeson), the creator of Doc Savage. In literary terms, most such melodrama is not particularly impressive, although a pulp hero endowed with superficial sophistication, like James Bond, can be considered a permissible vacation from reality.

With these two characters, Farmer found at hand a pair of heroes who had not only fascinated his own imagination in his youth, but shown enough endurance to appeal to later generations. The sixties had witnessed a new explosion of interest in both Tarzan and Doc Savage, with Ballantine reprinting the Tarzan books in paperback, and Bantam books doing the Doc Savage adventures. Both pulp heroes, therefore, were truly the centers of popular myths, especially Tarzan, who had already been adapted into numerous films, television shows, and comic books. If Doc Savage seems at first to have a lesser appeal to the popular imagination, it should be noted that

Farmer sees Savage as an early prototype of James Bond, who became the global hero myth of the sixties. Farmer's appropriation of these myths was to be an important stimulus for his imagination: the Tarzan and Doc Savage sagas became the source of several books. Farmer's use of the mythology will be examined in greater detail in a later part of this book. For the moment we are concerned with the imaginative transformation of Tarzan and Savage in *A Feast Unknown*, where Farmer's treatment of them is largely comic and satirical.

Here Farmer endows his larger-than-life heroes with larger-than-life sexual appeal. Theodore Sturgeon, a science fiction writer who has provocatively challenged taboos himself, notes in a perceptive "afterword" that pulp heroes generally followed careers that were extremely chaste or bowdlerized, since pulp editors were notoriously fearful of censorship, and almost obsessively wary about the inhibitions of their readers (whose intelligence they often underestimated). But, Sturgeon comments, the violence and carnage in the lives of pulp heroes like Doc Savage and Tarzan often seem to be a displacement of or substitution for what would be a prodigious sexual energy in less prudish hero sagas—an idea that other readers acquainted with psychoanalytic thought have sometimes voiced. Burroughs's Tarzan is, despite Burroughs's romanticism, a rather workmanlike killer, who far from showing civilized qualms about violence, usually celebrates his kills with the high decibel roar of triumph that Burroughs attributes to the "bull apes." In fact, as Richard Lupoff remarks in his 1965 study, *Edgar Rice Burroughs: Master of Adventure*, and as Farmer reaffirms in *Tarzan Alive*, Tarzan is essentially a savage and untamed personality, even in a tuxedo speaking with a flawless, upper-class British accent.

However, this untamed energy does not extend to Tarzan's sexual nature, at least in Burroughs' version of the saga. Tarzan's faithfulness to Jane is legendary. For example, although he travels around the globe and is frequently tempted by the sexual advances of seductive females, all highly charged with erotic symbolism, Tarzan always remains faithful to his first love, his wife, although her image as an erotic figure diminishes sharply in most of the later Tarzan books. On this subject, Burroughs, a child of the Victorian age, was not only shackled by the restrictions of editors, but clearly a prisoner of his own Victorian conventions. (We must observe, however, in fairness to Burroughs, that when he moved his stories to Mars in the John Carter saga, eroticism had a tendency to come closer to the surface: Dejah Thoris, John Carter's spouse, is virtually a female goddess archetype who may live for a thousand years. She is nude when Carter first meets her, although Burroughs later provided her and his other Martian women with some rather skimpy clothes.)

Victorian convention also fettered Doc Savage, surely one of the most sexless super heroes ever conceived. Unlike many of his contemporaries in the 1930s, Savage does not even have a romantic passion for a wife or sweetheart; the closest thing to a female lead in the series is his cousin Patricia, a superwoman with erotic appeal. To be sure, Patricia may entertain a passion for Savage, but his sexual energy seems to be almost entirely sublimated to virile action, or his passions for science and reforming criminals. Tarzan and Doc Savage are hardly alone among American heroes whose sagas have emphasized violence without sexuality. In fact, part of the importance of Tarzan and Doc Savage is the fact that they are typical of American heroic mythology, and hence of certain elements in the American psyche, at least until the advent of the 1970s.

The sexual emasculation of the American hero is the result of more than just a mental block in Burroughs, Dent, or their readers and editors. It has been a feature of American myths since the emergence of Cooper's Leatherstocking, whom D. H. Lawrence in *Studies in Classic American Literature* defines in terms of chastity and a complementary obsession with killing and death. Leslie Fiedler, influenced by Lawrence and Freud, has emphasized this theme at greater length in his important study, *Love and Death in the American Novel* (1960), citing a wide range of instances from Cooper, Melville, and Twain through the 1950s. Fiedler has argued that the male American imagination rebelled not only against conventional social life, but against woman and the feminine principle. In particular, Fiedler asserts, the masculine American writer felt revulsion against the explicit treatment of an erotic relationship with a female. Although not everyone accepts Fiedler's arguments, and although Fiedler tends to overstate his arguments in the classic tradition of the polemicist, there is much to support his views.

Incidentally, Fiedler's perception that Farmer, from the beginning of his career, sought to give a sexual dimension to his science fiction heroes is partly behind Fiedler's enthusiastic praise of Farmer's work in the essay mentioned earlier. Fiedler's review of *Tarzan Alive* alludes to *A Feast Unknown*, and defines part of Farmer's achievement as his imaginative revision of the Tarzan myth, particularly Farmer's innovative insistence on Tarzan's "extraordinary sexual endowment."

In short, then, *A Feast Unknown* is Farmer's most radical assault on sexual puritanism and American cultural archetypes. It is a work of immense vitality and imaginative energy, and an appropriate fruition of the rebellious and iconclastic spirit that was an essential part of Farmer's writing from the beginning. However, these comments about the work's energy should not distract attention from the book's artistry.

Though not particularly subtle, Farmer's satire is skillfully managed in *Feast*. The narrative strategy is clever, owing something to the Baker Street Irregulars. Farmer adopts the convention that he is publishing the secret memoirs of Lord Grandrith—supposedly Lord Greystoke's actual name—which candidly reveal Tarzan in the flesh, as opposed to the "romantic" distortions of Grandrith's "biographer," a reference of course to Burroughs. This strategy imparts a sardonic and anti-heroic tone to the narrative, as well as the illusion of shameless candor.

Farmer's major satirical gambit is to give Grandrith and Caliban large genitalia, with suitably involuntary reactions. For much of the narrative, Grandrith complains of suffering from a peculiar affliction: after each battle resulting in the death of an opponent, Grandrith enjoys an inexplicable involuntary erection followed by an ejaculation. Although this absurd condition is eventually cured and rationalized in Farmer's narrative through the work of a drug, Grandrith's sexual explosions are Farmer's way of suggesting the close relationship between repressed sexuality and the obsession with death in the hero myths he is satirizing. Doc Caliban, for a time Grandrith's antagonist in the book—although by mythological logic his half-brother—suffers from a similar malady. This constant stimulation of erotic organs makes both Grandrith and Caliban comic figures, and sets up the book's most memorable comic scene: a duel between Grandrith and Caliban fought with gigantic erections on a shaky suspension bridge in darkest Africa. Here Farmer creates an extremely funny parody of the single combat scenes in heroic films and pulp romances, battles usually waged between two superhuman heroes with weapons that are phallic substitutes, such as swords or guns.

Farmer's satiric narrative contains numerous mocking assaults on romanticized narrative conventions. For example, Grandrith's narration treats violence quite casually, not at all in the melodramatic tone of Burroughs or Dent. Engaged in an epic private war which begins in Africa and continues to his ancestral seat in England, he describes violence in a flatly realistic style, treating it as a necessary evil of his existence. Here Grandrith is depicted as something of an anti-hero, not burdened by illusions about fairness in fighting, or showing "humanitarian" sympathies toward the antagonists in his relentless vendetta.

Farmer also deflates Burroughs' sentimentalization of English aristocracy when Grandrith asserts early in the narrative that Jack the Ripper, one of English society's most feared psychopathic killers, was his actual father, despite Grandrith's supposed aristocratic heritage. According to Grandrith, the Ripper raped his noble mother in a hansom cab—so much for Tarzan's titled lineage! (In *Tarzan Alive*, Farmer was to make the same point more subtly by giving Tarzan a mad peer with proletarian sympathies as a grandfather.)

The pretense that Tarzan acts on the basis of civilized morals is treated with scorn. Grandrith scoffs at the idea that his consciousness is any way "civilized": his mind is completely an "African" one, he asserts, and "Africa" here clearly symbolizes a darkly primitive unconscious substratum of the human psyche, corresponding in psychoanalytic theory to the Freudian id or to the broader concept of the collective unconscious postulated in Jungian thought. Here Farmer touches a theme that preoccupies him in later treatments of the Tarzan mythos.

One of the most imaginative aspects of this novel is the depiction of Grandrith's grim opponents, his benefactors turned antagonists, the mysterious and sinister "Nine." These long-lived beings are supposedly secret manipulators of history, and possessors of the power of prolonged and renewed life. Sturgeon, in his illuminating Afterword, calls the "Nine" Farmer's "name for something which has preoccupied humanity since it could be called human. It is the awareness of a controlling Presence or Entity of immense resource, merciless power, and a set of inexorable aims against which we mortals (they, of course, are immortal) must be tested."

On the surface level of the narrative, the Nine are a secret group of leaders from various societies in Earth's ancient past who have lived thousands of years. Grandrith and Caliban are veterans of their arcane initiations given in a dark African cave to candidates for their group. But on a symbolic level, the Nine are an imaginative projection of the divinities or forces who control and renew human life, a mythological complex corresponding to the gods and fates in Greek mythology, to the dark divinities in some other mythologies, or to the powers in the unconscious half of the psyche in Jung's psychological theory. To suggest their primitive nature, Farmer depicts them as incredibly archaic, also an indication that, despite their potency, they are an "offense" to the supposedly enlightened consciousness of "civilized" man. It is obvious that Farmer, somewhat like Jung and D. H. Lawrence, sees the conscious mind of twentieth century technological man as out of touch with the deepest emotional centers in his unconscious.

At the heart of the book is a dark ceremony supervised by the Nine in a mountain cave of central Africa (probably a womb symbol), in which Grandrith and Caliban participate annually. This is the feast that celebrates a physical renewal of life and promises a longevity of 30,000 years. At this ritual, male and female genitalia are removed from sacrificial victims (their organs are later magically restored through drug-induced organic growth) and dismembered as a communal meal for the initiates. This dark pagan communion has mystic and ‹sacramental overtones, although its cannibalistic nature is, in Farmer's vivid description, shocking to the conventional consciousness. As a celebration of the renewal of vitality, it combines two of Farmer's most significant symbolic actions, eating and sexuality (as Fiedler has noted, sexuality takes on a sacramental quality in Farmer's work when combined with images of eating). Clearly, Farmer's imagination reaches deeply into the "forbidden zones" of the unconscious region of the psyche to describe this vivid and shocking scene. A comparable moment in serious literature is Hans Castorp's dream in the "Snow" chapter of Thomas Mann's *The Magic Mountain*, where the bright, smiling world of beautiful forms in a sacred grove is counterbalanced by a dark ritual of human sacrifice within an archaic temple. Like Mann, Farmer in *Feast* projects a vision of the biological basis of human life as a grim but exultant scene of human sacrifice. Both scenes affirm life, but in somewhat different ways. The vision of Mann's Castorp teaches him that all life coexists with an inevitable process of sacrifice and destruction. Farmer's scene of cannibalism suggests that human vitality must inevitably feed on life in order to be mystically renewed. Though Farmer is hardly an artist of Thomas Mann's stature, his imaginative power in the feast scene—and throughout most of this novel—is impressive.

An interesting transformation of Farmer's major characters, the narrator Grandrith, and Doc Caliban, takes place when the action moves to a denouement in the remote northwest of England, at Grandrith's ancestral home. Cured of his proclivity for erections after every act of violence, Grandrith begins to take on the identity of a more conventional epic hero. After learning the secret of their birth—they had the same father—Grandrith and Caliban are reconciled, with all misunderstandings forgotten. Now they join forces to become antagonists of the Nine whom they had formerly served: their mission becomes an effort to free humanity from the oppressive, dehumanizing dominance of these ancient masters. Thus they are transformed, or restored, to the position of heroes with a humanist purpose. Moreover, Grandrith, who has an absent wife called Clio (not Jane), becomes the lover of Patricia, Doc Caliban's beautiful cousin. In the original Doc Savage saga, Patricia Savage, a fantasy heroine of considerable erotic dimensions, was deprived of her sex life by Dent and his editors. In effect, Farmer has Tarzan (or Grandrith) rescuing Patricia, like some captive princess, from the celibacy enforced upon her by an inhibited author and editors. At the same time, on a symbolic level, Grandrith's relationship with Patricia, whom he accepts as an equal, affirms the Farmer hero's need—defined in earlier fiction—to accept the feminine principle in order to achieve wholeness.

Farmer's satirical treatment of romantic hero myths does not culminate in a final rejection of the mythology, but a transformation of it to a more sophisticated form. Curiously enough, the transmutation of the Tarzan and Savage myths reaffirms some of their inner meanings, while enlarging them to include an awareness of sexual realities.

A Feast Unknown is Farmer's boldest exploration of sexuality in his fiction, and undoubtedly one of his most interesting books. Although it is a work of rather crude vitality, it displays some accomplished artistry. Its comic gusto and ribald imagery make it a hard book to dislike, although no doubt some readers will find the violence in the story objectionable, even though the carnage is presented for satiric purposes. Although the book is unlikely to be read as widely as some other Farmer stories, it will no doubt maintain a following of enthusiastic and discerning readers.

The writing of *A Feast Unknown* seemed to bring to an end one phase of Farmer's career and point toward the beginning of a new one. If, in much of his fifties and sixties fiction, Farmer had persistently attacked dogmas and taboos of religion and sex, he saw, in 1969, society's attitudes changing in some of the directions his work had anticipated. His professional career had begun in a decade noted for its anti-intellectualism, and persisted through a decade enthusiastically receptive to social reform. Henceforward, Farmer's iconoclasm could be more readily incorporated into his effort to construct large personal myths in his fiction—as he would do in exploring the Tarzan and Savage mythos, and in resurrecting the Riverworld.

In *A Feast*, Farmer had begun the task of recovering the heroic mythology of Tarzan and Savage for fictional purposes. The rediscovery of this mythology was stimulating to Farmer's creative impulses, and the transformation and reinterpretation of these myths became central to the development of Farmer's fictional mythmaking in the seventies. In the next few years Farmer wrote a number of books exploring the Tarzan and Doc Savage myths; these will be covered later in this book. These works combined Farmer's intellectual interests with the narrative skills and trickster characters of the formula adventure novels Farmer had been writing, from *The Green Odyssey* (1957) through the late sixties. These works, to which we now turn our attention, show Farmer not only mastering his craft, but sketching the outlines of a mythology he would depict in sharper detail in the 1970s.

III
Trickster Heroes and Primitive Worlds

(1)

As an alternative to innocent heroes who are initiated into sexuality in such novels as *The Lovers* and *Dare*, Farmer had also begun using, as early as the mid-fifties protagonists who are clever, worldly wise tricksters. Among the first of these were Father John Carmody of the Carmody stories, and Alan Green of *The Green Odyssey*. In the sixties Farmer developed his trickster figures further, mainly with his hero Kickaha of the World of Tiers novels. Finally, the trickster hero would find his apotheosis in the Lord Greystoke of *Tarzan Alive* and other books.

Sometimes considered anti-heroes—although it seems better to reserve that title for the passive weaklings who appear in much modernist fiction—trickster heroes are fairly common in literary romances. In *The Secular Scripture*, Northrop Frye divides the heroes of romance into two types, those who rely on force and those who succeed by guile and fraud, the second type being a short definition of the trickster archetype. The trickster is also an important character in many primitive myths and legends. Even in primitive tales, however, the character may be exceedingly complex. In more advanced myth and literature, the trickster is very often a fascinating and complicated individual, as with the Norse god Loki and the Greek god Hermes. Odysseus is one of the immortal incarnations of the trickster in literature, although his feminine counterpart Penelope should not be overlooked. Medieval legend provides us with such trickster figures as Robin Hood, but the type is even more common in the tricky slaves and schemers of satiric comedy. As the rogue or *picaro* hero, the trickster survived the transition of European literature from the romance and epic of the Renaissance to the realism of the eighteenth century with its picaresque novels. The trickster hero was also a staple figure in American folklore and popular fiction long before his incarnation as a mischievous boy in *Tom Sawyer* and *Huckleberry Finn*. Tricksters continue to be sympathetic characters in American literature in such works as Faulkner's *The Reivers* and in popular fiction and films. But we must note that the trickster can also forfeit the sympathy felt for him, as, for example, when a trickster in political life is revealed as morally suspect and obsessed with perpetuating his power.

In turning to the trickster hero, then, Farmer obviously chose a durable type, renowned in both popular and classic literature. Such heroes helped to improve the quality of his formula adventure novels considerably by providing freshness and vitality. A hero who solves every crisis by flexing his muscles is likely to become boring, even on the most superficial level of reading. On the other hand, a hero who extricates himself from trouble by using quick wits is a challenge to the writer who can breathe new life into hackneyed plots. In fact, such mental sharpness is probably one of the main reasons that private eyes like Sam Spade and Philip Marlowe continue to fascinate readers.

It seems to be worth noting that the trickster mentality represents an important side of Farmer's personality. In the late sixties and early seventies, the creator of trickster heroes began to show readers that he could be a clever innovator with literary forms in "experimental" stories and parodies. Farmer's considerable gifts as a comic writer also reveal some of his own trickster skills.

(2)

Farmer's first trickster novel is *The Green Odyssey* (1957), produced not long after Farmer's unhappy experience with the original Riverworld novel. The frustration of Farmer's ambitions may have encouraged him to tackle a more conventional adventure story in order to get his career moving again.

The hero or anti-hero of *Odyssey* is Alan Green, an explorer (originally a marine food specialist) marooned on a backward planet of petty kingdoms and provincial religious cults. Green, pressed into slavery in the service of a decadent duke, and encumbered with a native wife, a daughter, and some step-children, longs to return to Earth. His chance comes when news of a ship from Earth landing at a distant city moves him to escape and set off on an overland trek to reach the terrestrials. After numerous amusing and picaresque adventures, Green completes his odyssey; but, unable to elude his wife and family, he must take them along. Despite the novel's title, Green is no wily Odysseus, for he frequently becomes the target of satire himself as he finds himself in one embarrassing situation after another. But Farmer's comic sense is a little uncertain in this book; the primitive or pre-industrial societies on the planet are depicted as quaintly ridiculous, with absurd gods and goddesses and unpronounceable names loaded with x's, z's and q's. Green, feeling the cultural superiority of twentieth-century technological man (especially the American middle-class male of the fifties), views the natives around him with patronizing contempt, although it is often his wife's intelligence which rescues him from his predicaments. Green's attitudes are credible enough, but it is not hard to conclude that they come rather close to the author's own belief at this time. Such a superficial view of a pre-technological culture seems shallow compared with Farmer's later work.

Green does show some growth in competence and moral outlook during the course of the novel. His schemes become more successful after his escape and his voyage across the great desert in a fleet of sailing wagons called "windrollers." Whereas in the beginning Green tries to evade his responsibilities as father and husband, at the end of the novel he vows to return to his family after a visit to Earth, and to devote the remainder of his life to improving conditions on his adopted planet.

In short, *The Green Odyssey* uses a classic comic situation, the escape of a tricky slave, and manages to be frequently amusing, while depicting moral growth in the hero. But the novel seems little more than a skillful entertainment in the mode of the 1940s science fiction by L. Sprague de Camp. Green seems less impressive as a trickster than his shrewd wife, Amra, and the novel, despite some anticipations of the later Farmer, remains a standard variation on the formulaic theme of the rogue abandoned on a distant planet.

Another early trickster figure is Father John Carmody, the itinerant priest of several fifties and sixties interplanetary stories. Carmody, whom we have already encountered in "Father" and the sixties novel, *Night of Light*, is a reformed rogue, a trickster who has painfully acquired a conscience (a process described in the first half of *Night of Light*). It is characteristic that Farmer's tricksters, though specialists in survival, usually develop a conscience or evince a code of values that makes them sympathetic. But there are differences among them. For instance, Farmer's Lord Greystoke is a grim, sardonic, implacable adventurer, while Kickaha, on the other hand, though wary and sceptical, often displays a heart of gold. Among these characters, Carmody is an exemplar of compassionate Christian humanist values, although Farmer himself is not a Christian, and *Night of Light* shows Carmody recognizing that there is an ambiguous character to religious faith.

Two Carmody stories illustrate Carmody as trickster moralist. In "A Few Miles" (1960), Carmody, a short, fat, middle-aged, unheroic man somewhat reminiscent of G. K. Chesterton's Father Brown, has been given his first assignment to the planet Wildenwooly, but no passage money to get there. Even reaching the space station where he should embark proves to be excruciatingly difficult, and Carmody finally becomes the victim of a large, earthbound bird called a "horowitz" which attaches a big leathery egg to his chest. This painful predicament can end only when the egg hatches, but Carmody, sustained by his faith, has a way of making the best of humiliating situations. The scientific community's interest in observing the offspring of the horowitz in its native habitat provides Carmody with a free ticket to Wildenwooly, as a reward for taking care of the egg during gestation. Thus, paradoxically, the priest, using guile, compassion, faith and sometimes good luck, is able to convert embarrassing predicaments to benefits to himself and his causes. Carmody attributes such reversals to divine providence.

"Prometheus" (1961), a sequel to "A Few Miles," effectively depicts Carmody as a compassionate and sophisticated Christian humanist. Waiting for the egg to hatch on the planet Feral, Carmody lives with a band of horowitzes, and, finding them capable of learning speech, teaches them their first language. With speech comes knowledge, for Carmody educates the better students among the younger horowitzes about human technology and culture. Eventually, Carmody as Prometheus proves to be a bringer not merely of fire, but of light, or moral enlightenment. Troubled by the lack of religion and an ethical code among the horowitzes, Carmody ponders the theological question of whether sentient animals have souls. A vision seen by one of the younger birds finally convinces him that the horowitzes are theologically on the same moral level as humans. Consequently, Carmody spends his final evening on the planet teaching the articulate birds some principles of Christian theology and a synthesis of the ethics and the Mosaic law derived from reflection on evolution. Although Carmody acknowledges to a fellow human that these ethical ideals will produce psychological conflicts for the sentient birds, he considers the presentation of theology and ethics to his students a completion of his role as Prometheus, or bringer of human awareness.

"Prometheus" embodies Farmer's theme that what used to be called "the soul" is acquired through an evolution of consciousness, dramatized here by the acquisition of spoken language, the development of the imagination (the ability to see visions), and finally the attainment of an ethical code. The story also portrays Carmody in the role of a liberal Christian moralist, willing to grant respect and spiritual equality to any sentient species (however grotesque it appears to humans) which demonstrates intelligence and the potential for ethical growth. As teacher and lawgiver, Carmody displays humility and Christian charity, a far remove from the power-obsessed bigots of *The Lovers* and the nervous puritan of "My Sister's Brother." Carmody is the trickster as moralist, one of the major figures in Farmer's fiction.

The Carmody stories often use paradox to reconcile theology and evolution, much as the Father Brown tales employ paradox to make detective stories exercises in moral theology. But perhaps the most interesting paradox of the Carmody stories is that Farmer, who rejects the Christian father, god and Christian theology in general, is able through Carmody to demonstrate a sense of Christian morality. Although an agnostic and a secular humanist at this time, Farmer shows great sympathy for the spirit of Christian ethics, at least in the Carmody stories and many of his important later novels.

(3)

In the sixties, Farmer began a formula adventure series for Ace Books that was to become fairly successful. These novels, less ambitious and less concerned with social criticism than Farmer's more speculative works, are notable mainly for some imaginative mythmaking and comic gusto. They also demonstrate Farmer's increasingly sure craftsmanship. The series introduces a character who is a favorite with Farmer himself and many of his readers—Kickaha, his most sympathetic trickster hero.

These novels, which have become known as the "World of Tiers" series, began with *The Maker of Universes* (1965). The appeal of the Tiers books is the ancient one of wish-fulfillment romance: they belong to the science fiction traditions of tales inspired by the desire to escape from the boringly commonplace world to a more lively or adventurous one. Such stories seldom receive much respect from critics unless they carry strong theological or philosophical weight, as with the Narnian Chronicles or Ursula Le Guin's Earthsea Trilogy. Farmer's Tiers novels do not belong in such distinguished company, but it is easy to appreciate their inventiveness and high spirits.

The Maker of Universes begins with a hero exasperated by a life of bondage to the commonplace. Robert Wolff, an aging, retired Ph.D with a nagging wife, is shopping for a suburban home in Arizona. Frustrated at the diminished possibilities of his life, Wolff discovers a new existence, when, while inspecting the house, he accidentally passes through a "gate" into another world. Thus Farmer follows one of the important principles of the romantic fantasy tradition by making the passage a welcome release from a disappointing or intolerable situation in this one. Wolff goes into one of a number of "pocket universes," or worlds in dimensions at right angles to our own. The "pocket universes" occupy a different position in space, on the basis of a principle easier to accept than to comprehend. Although it is some time before Wolff learns the truth, he finds that the pocket universes are ruled by a family of singularly unpleasant "Lords" or petty godlings, each of whom has power over a particular world. In fact, each lord has constructed his world as a kind of toy or play thing, using an elaborate advanced technology. The pocket universes are developed largely on the romantic primitive model, like so many of Farmer's other constructed worlds with large wilderness areas, nomadic tribesmen, barbaric cities, and even a tribe of American Indians transported there before they had a chance to be corrupted by whites. In other words, the pocket worlds, existing on a series of "levels," provide a playground not only for the villainous "lords," but also for Farmer's heroes as well, as Burroughs' Mars served John Carter.

The primitive nature of these worlds is counterpointed, however, by advanced technology characteristic of space opera. The Lords and some of the other characters use laser guns called "beamers"; some of the Lords have created monsters through ill-advised experiments; and the Lords build elaborate palaces full of electronic traps. Thus, in the Tiers novels Farmer skillfully creates entertaining escape narratives that combine the appeal of preindustrial cultures with post-twentieth century technology. Popular films like the *Star Wars* trilogy rely on similar devices.

Farmer also provides large dollops of satire and humor. One of the in-jokes for erudite readers is the naming of the "Lords," who are given the clumsy names of the divinities in William Blake's "prophetic" or visionary poems. Any reader who has struggled with Blake's Urizen, Tharmas, Vala, Palamabron, and so on, or who has conscientiously worked his way through some of the brilliant but complex commentaries on Blake, will surely appreciate Farmer's humor.

An even more sardonic concept is the Lords' unpleasant personalities: they are virtually without redeeming traits. Divinities and quasi-divine figures who control and manipulate human beings are nearly always ambiguous or simply evil in Farmer's work, with the exception of a few mother goddesses. God figures, from the "Father" of "Father" and Boygur of *Lord Tyger* to the Ethicals of the Riverworld, are sinister beings who would circumscribe human freedom and propagate mysteries by withholding truth. However, the Lords of the Tiers novels are perhaps the most obnoxious divinities in Farmer's fiction—or in anyone else's. Selfish, deceitful, cowardly, self-pitying, callous, and petty, they are indifferent to the fate of the creatures in their charge, if not actually malicious toward them. Human only in their faults, they cannot even achieve a Satanic level of grandeur. On the whole, their banal meanness suggests a group of jealous university administrators or corporate executives jockeying for power.

With such antagonists, it is easy to sympathize with any decent human characters in the series. But as *The Maker of Universes* unfolds, Wolff ceases to be an ineffectual senior citizen; endowed with a youthful physique, he soon develops a heroic stature and gradually remembers a pre-human past. Indeed, Wolff has been suffering from the amnesia that Northrop Frye describes as a frequent affliction of heroes at the beginning of romances. In the conventions of fairy tales, an unlikely character who wanders into the action usually turns out to be the central figure in a complicated plot, and eventually changing the world of the story. A similar logic operates in romantic fantasy: Wolff thus turns out to be Lord Jadawin, whom an enemy lord had relocated on earth, after having removed his memory. By the end of the novel, Wolff has recovered his identity and routed his enemies. Yet Wolff has been humanized by his existence on earth, and, unlike his fellow lords, he has learned to act with a human sense of morality.

Despite an effective plot stressing Wolff's moral growth, *The Maker of Universes* moves sluggishly until the middle of the story, when Farmer introduces his secondary hero, Kickaha. "Kickaha" is the Indian name of a rogue called Paul Janus Finnegan, originally from Terre Haute, Indiana. Of Irish and American Indian extraction, Kickaha had emigrated through a "gate" to the "World of Tiers" two decades before, in 1946, and is now blessed with perpetual youth. A cheerful trickster, he represents an affectionate projection of Farmer's own personality, and an idealization of Farmer's younger self (Farmer was twenty-eight in 1946). The identification of Farmer with Kickaha is quite obvious, for they share the same ethnic heritage, Hoosier origien, and initials. This has been confirmed by Farmer himself in various comments on his work: he contrasts Kickaha with the Farmer persona in the Riverworld, Peter Jairus Frigate. Kickaha is an idealized self, while Frigate is drawn with more realism, just as the Riverworld novels are more realistic than the Tiers series.

When Kickaha, a good-hearted knave who lives from moment to moment, comes into *The Maker of Universes* to assist Wolff, the book comes alive. Kickaha quickly becomes the most interesting character, taking the book away from Wolff. Wolff is a decent enough hero, struggling manfully against his handicaps and capable of some resourcefulness, but Wolff's struggle to find his identity and his concern for ethical behavior hampers him. Essentially, Wolff is a humorless hero, with a mind that lacks a philosophy. Clearly he cannot compete with Kickaha for the reader's attention.

It is not unusual for a secondary hero to take over an adventure series, but it took two more books before Kickaha was clearly established as the central figure of the saga. In *The Gates of Creation* (1966), he is absent—a wise move if Farmer hoped to keep Wolff from being eclipsed. Here Wolff finds himself in a trap with the other lords, all of them ensnared by Urizen, a demonic figure. Wolff displays cunning and strong leadership qualities in this trial, when he takes on the impossible task of guiding the group, and manages to bring them through numerous perils to a final liberation. There is much sardonic humor here, as Roger Zelazny has noted in a perceptive essay on the series, because the Lords, a group of unpleasant characters who detest each other, are forced to cooperate for mutual benefit: their predicament is grimly comic. The selfishness and treachery of the Lords, and their inability to cooperate for long, provides some ironic amusement before Wolff, according to formula, emerges triumphant.

Kickaha becomes the hero of his own novel in *A Private Cosmos* (1968) and thereby takes over the series, with Wolff virtually disappearing. *A Private Cosmos* is filled with lush natural landscapes and lively primitive characters. By now there has been a reversal of Farmer's perspective in *The Green Odyssey* a decade earlier, for savages and technologically backward peoples are portrayed sympathetically without being patronized. Signs of this reversal appear in earlier books, but the treatment of nature in *A Private Cosmos* suggests a new ecological awareness.

The conflict of the novel pits Kickaha against an inhuman life form, the "bellers"; but Kickaha is given an able ally in Anana, the sister of Wolff-Jadawin and hence a goddess herself. Anana is a dream woman of considerable sexual allure, relatively free of the obnoxious traits of the other lords.

Together they wage a battle agains the alien "bellers," the product of one of the lords' misbegotten experiments. Reminiscent of the menacing parasitic aliens from fifties science fiction, the bellers take over human bodies and minds in order to survive. Like the Orcs in Tolkien's *Lord of the Rings*, they are an enemy whose existence does not suggest covert hostility toward a particular race or ethnic group. Since the bellers are the products of a technology abused, their nature implies a criticism of the human tendency to use technology without considering the consequences.

As a hero, Kickaha is more fully realized here, having outgrown Farmer's original conception, as Falstaff probably outgrew Shakespeare's. In *A Private Cosmos*, Kickaha has become the exceptional athlete most men would like to be; a first-rate confidence man and imaginative liar who delights in his own tall tales; and a resilient adventurer with boundless energy. Despite his guile, Kickaha is generous and compassionate; he seems almost without malice, except for those enemies who richly deserve it. On the whole, Kickaha provides a comic tone in counterpoint to the melodramatic adventures of the Tiers novels. Indeed, Kickaha's stature is greater than the contrived adventures in which he appears.

After Kickaha and Anana successfully eliminate nearly all the bellers, Farmer rewards his hero with marriage to Anana and elevation to the pantheon of Lords. Another reward for Kickaha is a starring role in another book; but this entry in the series was not as enjoyable as the first three. *Behind the Walls of Terra* (1970) takes Kickaha and Anana to Earth in pursuit of the last beller. By now, Farmer's mastery of his craft is obvious, but he seems to be tiring of the series. At any rate, his new initiatives with the Riverworld material and the Lord Greystoke projects no doubt diverted his imagination from the Tiers series. As a result, *Behind the Walls of Terra* is the dullest novel in the saga. For the first half, there is some lively humor as Kickaha, returning to an Earth he had left in 1946, views the changes of twenty-five years with astonishment. When he is picked up by a rock group called "The Nome King and his Bad Eggs," the light-hearted satire is amusing. Kickaha reacts negatively to the smog and urban sprawl of the Los Angeles area of the late sixties, which Farmer also satirizes in *Image of the Beast*. But once the social observation ends, *Behind the Walls of Terra* flattens into some of Farmer's most boring writing.

After abandoning the series for several years to work on other books, most of them more challenging, Farmer returned to the World of Tiers with *The Lavalite World* (1977). This is perhaps the best novel in the series, with careful workmanship and detailed development of characters. As if to atone for *Behind the Walls of Terra*, Farmer describes the landscapes and primitive vistas of the lavalite universe in leisurely precision. Kickaha and his consort Anana pursue and are pursued by various enemies, and go through the usual cycle of capture and escape. Anana, however, is more fully developed as a character than before, and emerges as a heroic woman who is Kickaha's equal, rather than the secondary sex goddess of earlier books.

Beneath the melodramatic incidents of the plot, the novel displays the mythic theme of Kickaha returning to his Amerindian heritage as a lover of nature. In fact, the romantic rediscovery of nature is the real theme of the story, for the lush and unspoiled lavalite universe is as attractive a primitive world as Farmer has created. At the end of the novel, Kickaha and Anana are preparing to settle down and possess the lavalite world, like an Adam and

Eve granted an unending life in a second Eden. This wish-fulfillment ending consolidates the ecological vision that gradually emerges in the Tiers books and that flowers in this volume as a myth of nature recreated by the wise use of technology. The possibility of further books in the sequence remains, but if none is written, *The Lavalite World* can stand as a satisfactory finale.

Three other novels from the period of the early Tiers books contain trickster heroes and plots that fit loosely into the formula adventure pattern. These works show some family resemblances to the Tiers series, but their tone is more serious. ' Two have heroes of Amerindian extraction, like Kickaha, placed in new and challenging settings, while the third displays another interesting invented primitive setting. Indeed, inventive settings distinguish all three books; but, while trickster types, the heroes are not as memorable as Kickaha; and the narratives lack the liveliness of the Tiers books, without achieving a compensating moral or philosophical complexity.

The Gate of Time (1966) was first published in a shortened edition with an inappropriate title supplied by Belmont Books; it was later reprinted by Ace in a revised edition, with the cuts restored and some additional writing by Farmer, as *Two Hawks from Earth* (1979), Farmer's own title. This is an ambitious alternate world story. Roger Two Hawks, Farmer's hero, of Iroquoian and Nordic extraction, passes through a gate into another reality while flying a mission over Rumania in World War II. Like many Farmer heroes, Two Hawks must struggle to learn the nature of the world he is in, a situation that metaphorically reflects the human condition. At length Two Hawks finds himself living in a universe where the land masses of North and South America do not exist: hence humanity inhabits the Eurasian and African continents, but with vastly different societies and nationalities than those we know. Nevertheless, Two Hawks proves himself a competent hero and eventually makes a place 'for himself; he faces his predicament with the courage and practicality we expect of Farmer's best heroes. But the intellectual interest of the novel lies in the thoroughness and logic of Farmer's extrapolation of a different earth. One of the main postulates is that the Amerindians, instead of emigrating to America, were forced to turn inward to Asia and became mixed with European peoples. Farmer's extrapolation of the effects of this population movement on language and European culture is impressive. Although primarily an adventure novel, *Two Hawks from Earth* contains one of science fiction's more carefully worked out alternate worlds.

The Stone God Awakens (1970) also features a part-Iroquoian hero and some impressive extrapolations; but this novel would benefit from a revision similar to that given *Two Hawks*. The stone god is Ulysses Singing Bear, part Seneca and Onondaga, partly of Teutonic extraction, who awakens twenty million years in the future after being accidentally frozen to a stone-like condition while working on a biophysics experiment at Syracuse University. Farmer depicts the earth in this remote future as a post-technological environment where sentient creatures have evolved from cats, raccoons, squirrels, and bats. Humans are no longer the dominant species, though a few still exist. Singing Bear finds being a god to primitive tribes of cats and raccoons rather awkward, but eventually accepts a role as culture hero and providential leader to conduct his charges to a promised land. *The Stone God* offers some interesting speculations about the distant future, and contains some effective characters: Ghlikh, an obnoxious but amusing sentient bat, and Awina, a cat-woman, are well drawn, while Farmer manages to make even a giant thinking tree credible. But the novel shows evidence of careless writing; narrative time, for example, seems awkwardly handled. Although *The Stone God Awakens* has redeeming moments, it was one of five novels Farmer published in 1970, the year after he left his job to begin writing full time, and the book would have profited from some additional attention. Its shortcomings seem obvious when compared to the superior *Dark Is The Sun*, Farmer's 1979 novel of an even more remote future.

Even less successful is *The Wind Whales of Ishmael* (1971), an adventure sequel to *Moby-Dick*, starting with Ishmael dropping into another world after the Pequod disaster. Farmer's invention of flying whales in a world without seas is imaginative enough. In fact, hardly any Farmer novel lacks a rich stroke of invention, and the novel's premise must have seemed promising and challenging. But the Ishmael character is hardly Melville's poetic and philosophical seeker; rather, he resembles Melville's more casual sailor-adventurers in the early novels like *Typee*. Farmer gives Ishmael some ritual combats and allows him to settle down in what seems to be a vaguely Polynesian Arcadia with a native woman, a casually sketched heroine. But the action and characterizations not only lack vividness, but often appear underdeveloped. The novel's conclusion suggests that Ishmael's struggle is an effort to defeat the inexorable movement of time, but the action does not dramatize this theme. Its association with *Moby-Dick* makes the book a curiosity, but it is distinctly minor Farmer. The author himself does not rate the book highly.

In the trickster novels, especially the World of Tiers series and the three discussed above, Farmer developed his craftsmanship extensively, and began to shape a personal vision of heroism, uniting the trickster figure with the heroic primitive or noble savage archetype. The use of Amerindian ancestry for Kickaha, Two Hawks, and Ulysses Singing Bear shows a tendency to idealize the survival abilities and reverence for nature of the American Indian; moreover, Farmer no doubt hoped to improve the Indian's status in society by celebrating his heroic qualities. However, this mythic union of the idealized primitive hero or noble savage with the trickster archetype was to be more effectively achieved in the many books Farmer produced to transform the Tarzan mythology.

IV
The Tarzan and Doc Savage Mythos

(1)

Much of Farmer's writing in the early seventies is a series of variations on a theme, the re-interpretation of the "matter of Tarzan and Doc Savage." Farmer treats this material as a body of mythology similar to that of the Arthurian material, or, to take a parallel product of the American imagination, the mythology and legends of the Old West. Although the Tarzan and Doc Savage sagas have not received much attention from literary critics and scholars, they were rich with imaginative possibilities for Farmer. The very lowbrow and popular character of the mythology—together with its position on the fringes of American science fiction—helped make it attractive. On the one hand, there was the pleasure of mining and refining a lode of crude but rich popular myth; on the other, there were commercial possibilities in the large audience that these novels were reaching in the 1960s. Clearly, no professional writer who supports himself by his work can ignore the need for readers. Other writers like Lin Carter were beginning to exploit the Burroughs revival by writing unpretentious imitations of Burroughs' Martian romances. But what Farmer did with the Tarzan mythology was much more imaginative and intellectual, although at first it may have seemed that Farmer was merely writing a parody of pulp adventures.

One of Farmer's initial uses of the Tarzan-Doc Savage mythos after spoofing it in *A Feast Unknown* was simply to continue the adventures of Lord Grandrith and Doc Caliban in their epic struggle against the sinister Nine. The resumption of this conflict was presented in two 1970 novels for Ace Books, the paperback house that had published the "World of Tier" series. *Lord of the Trees* and *The Mad Goblin* were published in a single volume and describe concurrent quests by Grandrith and by Caliban and two of his partners. There is a certain symmetry to these novels, since the actions end at the same time and place (Stonehenge); but, despite being lively tongue-in-cheek melodramas, they do not advance Farmer's treatment of the material much beyond the level of *A Feast Unknown*. Grandrith and Caliban do not suffer the strange afflictions which affected them in *Feast*; indeed, unless one had read the earlier book, one would hardly imagine that these are sequels, since there is no explicit treatment of sex.

The better of the two is *Lord of the Trees*, simply because, like *Feast*, it is a first person narrative of Lord Grandrith, purporting to be another volume of his memoirs. Grandrith continues to be a sardonic narrator whose candid descriptions of violence and contempt for "civilized" hypocrisy display the "African" consciousness Farmer provides for him. By contrast, the Caliban novel is a third-person narrative, and Doc Caliban is viewed from the outside, with the emphasis of the story on melodramatic action. This contrast continues through Farmer's subsequent treatment including his fictional biographies. Whereas the recreation of Tarzan involved for Farmer the imaginative invention of Tarzan's mind as a contrast to the "civilized mentality," Doc Savage did not provide the same challenge. Tarzan's childhood and youth in the natural setting of the Arican jungle and grasslands gives him an appeal for which there is no counterpart in Doc Savage, as Farmer presents him.

These two adventure novels are rather amusing and "campy." No doubt Farmer could have gone on writing others in the Grandrith series if he had wished to exploit it commercially, but he had more innovative treatments of the two myths in mind. Northrop Frye in *The Secular Scripture* argues that sophisticated romancers are always turning to naive popular romances to remake them as more calculated and serious art, and Farmer sets out on ambitious transformations of his material in the fictional biographies of Tarzan and Savage.

(2)

Farmer has said publicly that he conceived the idea for *Tarzan Alive* (1972), the "definitive biography" of Lord Greystoke, from reading W. S. Baring-Gould's *Sherlock Holmes of Baker Street*. Baring-Gould's "biography" of Sherlock Holmes is a delightful book, faithful both to the letter and spirit of the Holmes tales—unlike most of the gimmicky Holmes pastiches of the seventies—recreating Holmes' career against the backdrop of the historical Victorian London. Often, Baring-Gould used his own imagination, as when he created a fictional childhood and youth for Holmes; there are also moments when the narrative achieves the suspense of the better Victorian Gothic novels. However, Baring-Gould's deft modern style would be never mistaken for any Victorian one, including A. Conan Doyle's. Nevertheless, the fusion of style and content is so happy that there is small wonder that this fictional biography encouraged Farmer to try a similar work

Interestingly enough, Burroughs' work had already been the subject of a non-fiction study, *Edgar Rice Burroughs: Master of Adventure*, by Richard Lupoff, reprinted by Ace in paperback. Lupoff, a talented science fiction writer, had written an examination of the Burroughs canon which is both a reader's guide and a critical assessment. With many interesting insights into Burroughs' attitude and popularity, Lupoff's work had demonstrated that Burroughs was by no means devoid of intellectual interest. Directed at a popular audience, the Lupoff book is intelligent and unpretentious, and deserves attention from any serious student of Burroughs' work. But though Farmer quotes from the Lupoff study in an epigraph, *Tarzan Alive* does not seem particularly indebted to it, other than sharing its subject.

A reader who comes to *Tarzan Alive* from Baring-Gould or Lupoff is likely to be impressed with Farmer's formidable task. The contrast with Baring-Gould and Lupoff is also apparent in the sheer imaginative scope of Farmer's book. For Holmes' career in the Doyle stories is rather consistent and repetitive despite minor lapses; even in Baring-Gould's narrative, it is largely confined to a period of forty years in a relatively stable Victorian and Edwardian England. Tarzan's career in the Lupoff book is rather sketchily described; besides being only one of Burroughs' fictional heroes, Tarzan in his later years is not of much interest to Lupoff.

By contrast, Farmer's Tarzan is conceived as a much larger mythic figure than even Burroughs was able to make him, and his life is set against the changing history of the globe, from the late Victorian age in 1888 to the post-World War II years, when Farmer expands the Tarzan saga beyond the limits of Burroughs' novels. Tarzan's adventures cut a wide swath in space and time, and Farmer makes an effort to enhance their epic magnitude by providing an immense backdrop of social history to complement them. Farmer emphasizes the changes in Tarzan's habitat, from a continent under the dominance of imperialist colonialism, to the Africa of the 1960s, with its emerging nations, unstable governments, and hostility to whites.

Moreover, Farmer enlarges Tarzan's stature by providing him with an extensive genealogy and table of family relationships. Tarzan's lineage is not only traced back through the descent of the Greystoke family, which Farmer ingeniously connects with actual English peers through playfully treating "Greystoke" as a disguised version of an authentic noble line; but Farmer goes even further connecting Tarzan with outrageous impudence to various literary characters, and through Scandinavian forebears to the Teutonic god, Odin. Thus, like the greatest heroes of myth, Tarzan is descended from a god! As for his contemporaries, Tarzan is shown to be related to most of the major heroes of popular fiction in the first half of the twentieth century. Here Farmer simply employs the logic of the mythmaking poet, who at a certain stage in the development of a mythology takes on the job of consolidating and rationalizing a number of loosely connected stories into a more coherent pattern, elevating heroes and gods to a pantheon.

At the same time that Farmer enlarges Tarzan's mythic image, he also attempts to make the story of Tarzan—which, despite some gross improbabilities, has enormous imaginative appeal—somewhat more realistic and scientifically credible. Such an enterprise involves amending many oversights of Burroughs as well as correcting or providing some kind of plausible explanation for some of Burroughs' absurd gaffes.

Farmer adopts two amusing strategies for correction of Burroughs. Since, like Baring-Gould, Farmer blandly pretends to work from the premise that Tarzan was a "real" person and Burroughs merely his biographer, Farmer often attributes certain of Burroughs' claims to Burroughs' innate "romanticism." For instance, Burroughs' reticence about Tarzan's puberty, and Burroughs' insistence that Tarzan always showed consistent fidelity to his wife throughout his global adventures, are explained as sentimental falsifications resulting from Burroughs' Victorian upbringing. On the other hand, Farmer impishly suggests that at times Burroughs changed the events of Tarzan's life to suit his narrative purposes because Burroughs needed to conceal the fact that Tarzan was an actual person: paradoxically, Burroughs wanted his reader to think he was writing ficion, and thus he deliberately violated credibility! Because of the interplay of such witty rationalizations, *Tarzan Alive* is often an immensely funny book.

One of the most fascinating aspects of Burroughs' Tarzan saga is the description of Tarzan's childhood and youth as a member of a tribe of "great apes," followed by Tarzan's gradual discovery of his civilized heritage through his father's books. In this story, Burroughs touched many deep mythic levels of the unconscious mind: Tarzan is like any divinely chosen prince living in obscurity and gradually discovering his powers and his identity (Arthur and other analogies will suggest themselves); and the narrative affirms certain basic human wishes about the ability of mind and will and heredity to transcend environment. However skeptical we may be, we all have a deepseated desire to believe that Tarzan could teach himself, completely without instruction, to read a language he had never spoken, in books largely about a civilization he had never seen. And, of course, there seems to be a human need to think that a child could survive in a natural environment with only animals for companions; at any rate, the legends of such survivals are widespread.

Farmer sets out to preserve these major themes of survival and self-discovery in the wilderness by combining his considerable scholarship with some boldly imaginative alterations of Burroughs' basic tale. Perhaps Farmer's master stroke in making the Tarzan story more credible, while preserving its basic appeal, is Farmer's explanation for Tarzan's remarkable life among the "apes." Any intelligent reader of *Tarzan of the Apes* soon learns, if he consults an encyclopedia, that Burroughs described Tarzan as being reared among a species of "great apes" which does not exist except in Burroughs' imagination. These "great apes" are more intelligent than gorillas or baboons, and they have a developed spoken language which the higher simians lack (the orangutan might be closest to Burroughs' idea). Essentially writing a fantasy to embody a personal myth, Burroughs surely was an author naively influenced by nineteenth century evolutionary mythology: he gave more human intelligence to the apes than they possess because they were supposed to be man's nearest kin in the animal kingdom. Burroughs' work is filled with evolutionary mythology about survival of the fittest and the extraordinary virtue of primitive man; in this respect his work is not much different from that of Kipling, Jack London, and many other writers of his time, including some with high reputations. But were there a species of apes like those Burroughs imagines, Tarzan's jungle childhood would become considerably more credible, even if some objections still remain.

Farmer deals with this problem by creating a fictional equivalent of such a species, although insisting that Burroughs misunderstood or concealed its true nature. The "great apes" were in reality a tribe called "the people," a humanoid species who represent the "missing link" postulated by evolutionary theory. Thus Tarzan was not reared by "apes" but by primitive human beings, perhaps the descendants of an original source group of humanity. Farmer then speculates that Burroughs probably concealed the truth to protect "the people," who were on the verge of extinction. These primitive humans have not been discovered in our time, of course, because they have conveniently died out.

With this explanation, many of the difficulties of Burroughs' narrative, including Tarzan's facility with language, are eased, if not completely eliminated. Farmer's creative revision of Burroughs here is a representative example of his method for increasing the credibility of the Tarzan saga. Of course, as we have noted, Farmer is really playing a very sophisticated game; and our pleasure in reading is largely derived from our enjoyment of the game. These rational explanations of Burroughs' outrageous absurdities are to be read with a sense of playful irony, much like that we often bring to reading the "argument" presented in a poem by a seventeenth century metaphysical poet such as John Donne or Andrew Marvell. We know that the argument will be an exercise in tortuous ingenuity, but we take delight in the author's mental gymnastics.

Burrough's careless writing produced some appalling inconsistencies, some of them formidable challenges even for a man with Farmer's prodigious powers of imagination and extrapolative logic. Consider the most notorious instance, the confusion of the time involving Tarzan's son. In *The Son of Tarzan*, Burroughs' fourth Tarzan novel, Tarzan's son Jack, supposedly born in 1912, is kidnapped, escapes, goes off to the jungle at age ten, and reenacts his father's heroic experiences for six years, eventually becoming known as "Korak the Killer." Then Tarzan returns to Africa and finds Korak, now a grown man with a sweetheart. However, in two succeeding volumes set during the First World War and in 1919, Jack is already an adult fighting for the allies; he later goes to Pal-ul-don, a mythical realm in central Africa, to rescue Tarzan and Jane. How did the baby of 1912 become the Korak of these books?

In the dream world of Burroughs' fiction, time could expand magically: the years from 1912 to 1914 were able to stretch elastically to contain Jack's childhood, youth, and passage to manhood. But Farmer, the biographer, must recast Burroughs' fiction to the constraints of historical time. Farmer's solution is to provide Tarzan with two sons, the baby of 1912 and an adopted one, a cousin called Jack Drummond in Farmer's version, who became "Korak the Killer" in *Son of Tarzan*.

At times, however, even Farmer's combination of ingenuity and logic is checkmated. Much of Farmer's narrative rationalizes and recasts events from Burroughs' long succession of twenty-four Tarzan novels. But with Volume XIII, *Tarzan at the Earth's Core*, dealing with Tarzan's journey to the land of Pellucidar, which Burroughs placed inside the Earth, even Farmer's imagination cannot provide a convincing rationale. An inner world within the Earth, though treated as a possibility by Jules Verne (probably Burroughs' source for the idea), is simply not credible today. Farmer is forced to concede that the novel is "all fiction, though very good fiction." He explains the book as a dream vision of Tarzan in a world of jungles and prehistoric animals, an unfallen natural paradise for a hero of Tarzan's capabilities.

Not only does Farmer revise Tarzan's career as depicted in the Burroughs books, but he extends it to the present, for, following the plot in a late Tarzan novel, Farmer confers immortality on Tarzan as the result of a treatment from an African witch doctor. In the last section of the biography Farmer brings the Tarzan saga up-to-date by imagining Tarzan becoming ever more cunning and wary in the treacherous late twentieth century. Even in the jungle, Tarzan had been a trickster. But in the jungle of international finance, in a changing Africa of nationalisms and race hatreds, and in a contemporary world that seeks to exploit or destroy the primitive, Tarzan becomes masterful about concealing his identity and masking his actions. As he brings his biography to a conclusion, Farmer turns from the expository rhetoric of the biographer to the narrative mode of the novelist, and describes Tarzan's expedition to remove a cache of gold from the ruins of Opar to a safer hiding place. Here we recognize that Farmer has not only fulfilled his purpose in the book, but justified his title. Tarzan has become alive for the reader once more, not just as a character in narrative but as the hero of a living myth.

What does the myth mean in Farmer's interpretation? *Tarzan Alive* makes it abundantly clear that the Tarzan story embodies two archetypal themes. First, Tarzan is an avatar of the trickster archetype, the hero who occurs in much primitive myth studied by anthropologists (Farmer cites Paul Radin's study, *The Trickster*), and already celebrated in Farmer's fiction, especially the Tiers novels. Farmer is here calling attention to an essential element of Tarzan's character in Burroughs, although it is a trait often overlooked or not developed in such popular adaptations as the Tarzan films. Tarzan's trickster qualities are, in fact, part of his appeal for Farmer, an essential aspect of Tarzan's character. Not surprisingly, Farmer portrays Tarzan as the supreme trickster, a hero skeptical about the laws of civilization and ready to bend them to his own uses to protect himself or those he loves. It is Tarzan's trickster guile that not only allows him to adapt, in appearance, to civilized life in his role as an English peer, but also enables him to cope successfully in business as a shrewd financial manipulator.

At the same time, Tarzan incarnates for Farmer the romantic noble savage myth descending from Rousseau. Hence, given the more liberated sexuality and pragmatic ethics Farmer provides him, Tarzan is in many ways a perfect hero for an author whose work contains, as we have seen, a very large spirit of romantic rebellion and criticism of society's fear of sex.

However, the Rousseau myth of the noble savage is a much larger matter than the championing of sexual liberation. For instance, it has usually been associated with a mystical sense of the fecundity and healing powers of nature. The myth has haunted the European and American imaginations since the eighteenth century; in America, it influenced the work of J. Fenimore Cooper, Herman Melville, Mark Twain, and Jack London in various ways, although it by no means received full allegiance from any of these. One of the primary meanings of the Rousseauist myth is the sense of a great vitality, freedom, and reverence for life among primitive peoples close to nature; and despite the hostility of many anti-romantic literary critics and scholars, the myth seems to be finding wider acceptance from intellectuals as well as from society in modern times, when our technological civilization threatens either to destroy us or to drive us insane.

In his revision and renovation of the Tarzan myth, then, Farmer joins the tradition of American writers who have idealized the challenge of the primitive experience and the values associated with primitive peoples, although Farmer views primitivism in a more skeptical way than naive romanticism. Not that Farmer makes a new departure with *Tarzan Alive*; he merely consolidates into a myth certain thematic concerns that had appeared earlier in his work, as for instance in "The Alley Man," and in his Kickaha novels. But this is as good a place as any to point out that Farmer's fiction, despite Farmer's great respect for science and technology, differs quite strongly from that of the previous generation of science fiction writers. Where Isaac Asimov's writing, for example, celebrates an ever increasing world of technology, Farmer's novels portray worlds where the claims of nature and man's benefiting from the experience of nature are recognized. In fact, Farmer's mythic constructions of the Tiers worlds and the Riverworld seem to be intended as syntheses reconciling nature and technology. However, this comment should not be taken to mean that Farmer espouses an uncritical romanticism about primitive life: a naive romancer like Burroughs may well celebrate nature and primitivism in book after book, but Farmer's sense of the relationship of nature and technology is more complex.

If Farmer successfully transforms the Tarzan myth in *Tarzan Alive*, then our final judgment of the "biography" must recognize it as one of Farmer's most successful works of fiction. Its uses of narrative form and imaginative interpretation of event are quite an innovation in Farmer's writing, even though he had models of the fictional biography to follow (Northcote Parkinson's Hornblower "biography" as well as Baring-Gould). *Tarzan Alive* is also an excellent example of Farmer's considerable scholarship, and it provided a compensation for the frustration of Farmer's ambition to be a biographer (one of his cherished hopes was to write a life of Richard Burton, before the task was ably performed by others). But we should not overlook the fact that the fictional biography is in the last analysis a work of fiction, a novel in an unusual form, and all Farmer's scholarship is finally subordinated to Farmer's purposes as a novelist. One of Farmer's most imaginative works, *Tarzan Alive* is also a first-rate display of his talent for the comic, with its parodies of scholarship and its wonderfully ingenious displays of logic. A case could also be made for the work as "experimental" fiction, similar to the avant garde post-modernist fiction written in the late sixties and seventies by writers influenced by Jorge Luis Borges, including John Barth and Thomas Pynchon, among others. Farmer has not been unaware of the "experimental" fiction written by serious writers, as we shall see when we examine some of his recent short stories. But to put *Tarzan Alive* into this category might be to adopt the ingenious logic Farmer uses to explain Burroughs, and also to do the book a disservice; for the new fiction, or anti-fiction, as some would have it, has been often associated with pretentiousness and facile cleverness. Farmer's easy mastery of a popular style and lack of pretense are major virtues of *Tarzan Alive*.

An important pendant to the Tarzan biography is a fictional "interview" with Lord Greystoke that Farmer published in *Esquire* in 1972 (and later reprinted in *The Book of Philip Jose Farmer*, 1973). This encounter, supposedly occurring in Gabon (where Farmer locates Tarzan's birth), recapitulates some of the themes of the biography; but it also depicts the sardonic and alienated personality that Farmer attributes to Lord Greystoke. For Farmer Tarzan is more than a hero myth; he is a clearly defined personality who speaks for natural and primitive values, and voices some of Farmer's criticisms of civilization. For Farmer's fictional recreation of Tarzan is not, most of the time, an indulgence in parody or literary horseplay, but part of his effort to transform and reshape the myth. The interview with Greystoke gives expression to Tarzan's personality more directly than the biography which focused on Tarzan's actions. Thus the interview is both entertaining and an addition to the portrait of the hero that Farmer is drawing.

(3)

A sharp contrast is clear between the vivid personality Farmer provides for Greystoke, and Farmer's treatment of Tarzan's American cousin, Doc Savage, in *Doc Savage: His Apocalyptic Life* (1973; revised edition, 1975). The success of the biography of Tarzan no doubt encouraged Farmer to turn to a fictional life of Savage, the other titan of *A Feast Unknown*, and an equal enthusiasm of Farmer's early escapist reading. Moreover, Farmer had shown in *Tarzan Alive* that his interest in heroic myth was that of a sophisticated scholar, influenced by many modern thinkers, including Joseph Campbell's attempt to establish an archetypal hero myth, *The Hero With a Thousand Faces* (1948). It is worth noting that one of Farmer's more perceptive academic critics, Russell Letson, has commented favorably and cogently on Farmer's interest in hero myths and the influence of Campbell, in an article in *Science Fiction Studies*, 4 (March 1977). Thus it was consistent with Farmer's interest in creative mythography for him to continue his transformation of pulp hero saga with his fictional biography of Savage.

In theory, Farmer attempts to treat Doc Savage as a reversal of the noble savage myth of Tarzan: although a physical giant, Savage is civilization's scientific savior. As saviors always must, he suffers loneliness and a sense of isolation from the people. He has to be ready for those "who would daily crucify him." Unfortunately, Savage seldom seems to be this three-dimensional personality in Farmer's book. Instead, he seems more like an overgrown Tom Swift with his laboratory and gadgets perched high over the streets of Manhattan.

Although written in a lively style, much of the biography discusses Savage's world rather than Savage himself. Separate chapters are given to Savage's comrades, since Savage heads a team of heroes with eccentric personalities. Farmer also provides an elaborate description of Savage's laboratory and weapons. The book contains some valuable research on Lester Dent, the author of most of the Savage stories, under the "house name" of Kenneth Robeson. Farmer's command of the one hundred eighty-one episodes of the Doc Savage saga is impressive, as is his scholarship in other areas touched by the Savage tales. But for all this, the Doc Savage biography turns out to be a good deal less interesting than *Tarzan Alive*. There would seem to be some obvious reasons. For one thing, the saga of Doc Savage probably possesses less imaginative appeal than Tarzan; not only is Savage a limited personality, but he is really neither a product of the city or the jungle, although he may move in both spheres of action. Instead, Savage is an incarnation of the naive faith in technology that has been characteristic of our civilization—and costly to our environment. Moreover, Savage's "apocalyptic" life fails to be genuinely apocalyptic, at least in the sense that visionary literature is apocalyptic, by changing our fundamental point of view about reality. Finally, Farmer does not transform and reinterpret the Savage myth as effectively as he did the Tarzan myth.

Although the Savage biography is a less interesting book than *Tarzan Alive*, its opening chapter is a fascinating tribute to the Savage stories as a modern myth, and the forcefulness of Farmer's writing in that chapter makes it a rhetorical *tour de force*. Throughout the book, Farmer's style is notable for its sustained vigor and wit, and Farmer's mastery of the Savage canon and the science involved in it displays an urbane erudition.

If it is not quite the successful remaking of popular myth that Farmer achieved in *Tarzan Alive*, *Doc Savage: His Apocalyptic Life* does establish Farmer as probably the supreme authority on the Doc Savage myth. Farmer's status as an authority on Savage is underscored by his having been commissioned by Warner Brothers to write a screenplay for the second Doc Savage film. Farmer completed the screenplay with enthusiasm in 1975, happy at the chance to employ his talents for a medium which he had always admired. But since the film was never produced, the merits of the screenplay remain unknown, although Universal has picked up an option on it. Unfortunately, the first Doc Savage film, a George Pal Production for Warner, was not very impressive and was quickly relegated to the limbo of TV reruns. This rather self-conscious and campy treatment of Savage and his comrades portrayed him as a pale imitation of James Bond, with the moral code of a boy scout. By 1974, the market for yet another spoof of Bond was at rock bottom, and the science fiction film had not yet achieved its renaissance with *Star Wars*. It is to be hoped that Hollywood will some day give Farmer's screenplay a chance, or that the film industry will be wise enough to make use of Farmer's considerable gifts for another film.

(4)

In *Tarzan Alive*, Farmer unified the mythology of Tarzan and Doc Savage, and expanded it to include numerous nineteenth-century literary characters including Elizabeth Bennet and Fitzwilliam Darcy from Jane Austen's *Pride and Prejudice*, by means of an elaborate genealogical table. This genealogy also links Tarzan and Savage with Sherlock Holmes and such famous twentieth-century fictional heroes as Lord Peter Wimsey and Travis McGee. The entire family of mythic heroes and heroines is traced back to a purported landing of a meteorite near Wold Newton in England in the early nineteenth century.

Radiation from the meteorite supposedly affected the occupants of three nearby horsedrawn coaches, all of whom contained women who were pregnant; and the family of heroes in the mythology are therefore descended from the mutated offspring produced after this incident. Hence some readers of Farmer have adopted the name "the Wold Newton series" to describe the books employing Farmer's revision of the Tarzan and Doc Savage mythology. The name is convenient enough, although the Wold Newton label does not include *Lord Tyger*, one of Farmer's most significant works inspired by the Tarzan myth.

The "Wold Newton" family connects the Tarzan and Savage biographies to a novel that borrows from Jules Verne rather than Burroughs or Lester Dent. *The Other Log of Phileas Fogg* (1973) attempts to revise Verne's *Around the World in Eighty Days* into a novel whose external events conceal a massive struggle of intrigue between two intergalactic forces. This ingenious narrative also involves the *Eighty Days* characters with Captain Nemo and Sherlock Holmes. But the book seldom comes to life. Too much of the novel is devoted to contrived explanations of the arcane meaning of the behavior of Verne's characters. Of necessity, the book is more expository than dramatic, and, of course, it suffers by comparison with the novel that provided its inspiration.

The "Wold Newton" family relationships are also in the background of a more spirited minor work, *The Adventure of the Peerless Peer* (1974). This is Farmer's excursion itno the well-populated land of Sherlock Holmes pastiche and parody. Holmes is one of Farmer's passions. Farmer regards Holmes as one of the most important popular heroes of the last hundred years, along with Tarzan and Savage, and various connections between the Holmes stories and Tarzan's life are established in *Tarzan Alive*. Later Farmer became the founder and tutelary spirit of the Peoria Sherlock Holmes Society, "The Hansoms of John Clayton," named for the cab driver in *The*

Hound of the Baskervilles whose name provides Farmer with an amusing link between Holmes and Tarzan. Thus a Farmer parody of Holmes was virtually inevitable.

Unlike most seventies Holmes novels (many of them ill-advised hackwork depending on commercial gimmicks that Lester Dent might have scorned), Farmer's novel is an unpretentious parody. There is no attempt to intellectualize Doyle, improve on his plots, or somehow "modernize" the moral outlook of his characters by using superficial Freudianism, as in *The Seven Per Cent Solution* and some of its progeny. While Farmer might not agree with Doyle on every issue, he has the professional's respect for another professional's work, and great admiration for Holmes' moral sense and intellectual abilities. To attempt to "improve on" works that represent a great achievement in a specific genre is somewhat different from revising the pulp mythology of Burroughs or Dent, and Farmer treats even these authors with considerable respect. The effort to "revise" Holmes by changing Holmes' character is an aberration of our anti-heroic age. For Farmer, it would not be "sacrilege" exactly, but a failure of esthetic tact, or just plain bad judgment. Farmer's Holmes parody is thus an act of homage to the Doyle canon, not a debunking or revisionist effort.

In *The Peerless Peer*, Holmes and Watson are dispatched to Africa by the British government during the First World War, encounter Lord Greystoke there, and also take an enchanting glance at the luscious white goddess, La of Opar, as she conducts some primeval rites in the nude. Aside from these long lingering looks, however, the action is chaste and restrained. The famous titans, Holmes and Tarzan, appear from Dr. Watson's bemused perspective as unpredictable comic figures. Tarzan in particular disturbs Watson with his primitive and un-English way of looking at things. Watson's own point of view as a beef-eating, common-sense Englishman is itself being gently satirized, of course.

In place of Doc Savage, *The Peerless Peer* offers another of the Wold Newton family, Richard Wentworth, or "The Spider," a nearly forgotten aviator and crime-fighting hero of the thirties pulps. Wentworth's humorless intensity appears to be a kind of insanity to Dr. Watson and the reader. Farmer's caricatures of Wentworth and Tarzan are modest but effective comic achievements.

On the whole, *The Peerless Peer* is a lightweight book, a broad but gentle parody of hero myths. Yet the novel succeeds within its own limited terms. It not only admits Farmer to the distinguished company of successful parodists of Doyle, from Mark Twain to Tom Stoppard, but it also displays Farmer's ability to spoof his own fiction about Lord Greystoke.

(5)

The Tarzan myth is extended in *Time's Last Gift*, a novel that provides Farmer's Tarzan with a new dimension. Of course, in the Lord Grandrith series, Farmer had put Grandrith in an epic struggle against the sinister Nine, but this conflict was rather melodramatic and did not allow Grandrith much opportunity to play a more positive role as humanist benefactor of mankind. *Time's Last Gift* tries to create a more humanistic career for Tarzan.

In *Time's Last Gift*, Farmer makes Gribardson, his Tarzan figure, a time traveler fascinated with the human past, a sometime Prometheus who has brought enlightenment to the people encountered there. However, this is not revealed immediately. The novel begins as a conventional time travel tale: an archeological expedition of four scientists in 2070 A. D. journeys to the world of 12,000 B.C. to learn about the origins of the human species. It is worth noting that in his only time travel novel thus far, Farmer dismisses the usual paradoxes of such narratives as illogical. Not all would agree, but many claim the paradoxes are tired conventions wisely ignored.

Beginning as a study of character relationships, *Time's Last Gift* uses the familiar motif of scientists stranded in a primitive world and undergoing personal conflicts. Two of the four scientists are a husband and wife, Drummond and Rachel Silverstein, whose marriage is strained. Although Rachel wants to be a dutiful wife, her task is made difficult by her husband's insecurity and fear of failure. Inevitably, her emotions are aroused by the mysterious John Gribardson, not only stronger physically and emotionally than her husband, but more sensitive to her feelings. Nor is her conflict eased by her husband's obvious jealousy. So far the novel seems to be heading toward an emotional climax resulting in an adulterous affair; but the human drama recedes into the background when Gribardson is revealed as the authentic Lord Greystoke and an experienced visitor to the past. Since the latter half of the novel is devoted to revealing Gribardson's earlier exploits as a time traveler, the human conflicts fade into insignificance. In essence, Farmer abandons the fiction of human relationships for heroic myth.

Farmer's depiction of Gribardson's past time travel adventures is largely expository. It is revealed that Gribardson has enjoyed various love affairs with women in different eras; has sired numerous children; and often played Prometheus for his fellow humans. The account of Gribardson's activity is fairly interesting, but it is not well dramatized. Clearly Farmer has enlarged Tarzan's sphere of action to include most of human history. Yet *Time's Last Gift* remains a disappointing novel. It depends too much on Farmer's transformed Tarzan myth, in *Tarzan Alive*, and not enough on its characters and their actions. It is important, however, as a prologue and background for the Opar novels. These books return to 12,000 B.C. to recreate Opar, the lost city discovered by Tarzan in *The Return of Tarzan*, which plays an important role in several Tarzan books. Although Burroughs filled the Tarzan novels with lost races, Opar and its archetypal white goddess La, always hopelessly in love with Tarzan, was Burroughs' most potent adaptation of H. Rider Haggard's lost race and white goddess myth (presented definitively in *She*).

In *Tarzan Alive* Farmer tried to set the Opar myth on a more rational foundation, as he did with many of Burroughs' compelling dream images. Burroughs had explained Opar as a colony of Lost Atlantis, somehow planted in central Africa. Farmer, however, dismisses Burroughs' explanation as a conventional rationalization. Instead, Farmer asserts, Tarzan's ruined Opar was the remnant of a prehistoric white civilization in central Africa's Chad basin. In *Tarzan Alive*, Farmer refers to this lost realm as the Chadean civilization. In the Opar novels, however, the lost civilization becomes the Khorkarsan empire, of which Opar was a late colony on a central African lake. Moreover, Farmer provides the Khokarsan world with a detailed imaginary history.

Important events in Khorkarsa's legends are the occasional visits of a godlike figure called "Sahhindar," who is the Tarzan, or Gribardson of *Time's Last Gift*. Sahhindar also makes brief and enigmatic appearances in the Opar novels themselves, altthough Farmer does not allow him to become a providence or *deux ex machina* for his characters. Although the presence of Sahhindar or Tarzan broods over the Opar novels, they are primarily concerned with the epic struggle of Hadon, the last hero from Opar at the time of what seems to be the empire's dissolution.

Hadon of Ancient Opar (1974) begins the saga. The novel describes Hadon's initiation and growth as he leaves his native city, goes to the imperial capital, competes successfully in the imperial games, but runs afoul of political intrigue between the emperor, corrupted by too much power, and his daughter, the priestess of Kho, the mother goddess. Traditionally, and in its most prosperous times, Khokarsa has followed the worship of a mother goddess; but occasionally decadent rulers have tried to assert the claims of Resu, a father and warrior god. In his madness, the decadent Minruth wants to overthrow the power of the mother goddess completely and establish masculine supremacy through a line of priest-emperors of Resu. Thus the Opar series continues Farmer's theme of associating human sanity and wholeness with the recognition of the feminine principle.

Sent on an absurd expedition to the northern parts of Africa by Minruth, Hadon shows extraordinary powers of leadership, and returns to Khokharsa with important discoveries, and with a woman who will become his wife. Lalila, the heroine, is a blond "white goddess" or earth goddess archetype, already the victim of a miscarriage from a brief mating with Sahhindar. Hadon's ambitions turn from political power to protecting Lalila, soon pregnant with his own child. The Khokharsan empire collapses into civil war on Hadon's return to the capital, because Minruth, who embodies the masculine principle gone insane, tries to overthrow the goddess Kho and have himself declared immortal. The novel concludes with Hadon attempting a desperate and perilous journey to take Lalila to his native city.

Flight to Opar (1976) continues the series with the narrative of Hadon's journey, the struggle intensified by Lalila's pregnancy. To fulfill an oracle, the child must be born in Opar. By now an accomplished trickster as well as a splendid swordsman, Hadon succeeds in reaching Opar by the combination of courage, prowess, and guile that other Farmer heroes usually display. The daughter of Hadon and Lalila is born under the protection of the goddess, and revealed to be La, the long-lived white goddess of Burroughs' Tarzan stories.

These Opar novels are solidly crafted formula adventures, with many credible characters. The romanticism of the series is counterpointed by frequent touches of sardonic irony. Lalila, the heroine, is a well-conceived character, both a credible woman and an attractive incarnation of the feminine principle. Although the Opar novels do not transcend the formula adventure tradition, they are superior examples of it. They show Farmer's ability, once again, to construct a primitive world in rich and complex detail, and his continuing assertion of the primacy of the feminine principle. At least one more novel in the series is planned.

(6)

Among Farmer's books inspired by the Tarzan myth, *Lord Tyger* (1970) is in a class by itself. With *A Feast Unknown* and *Tarzan Alive*, it is also one of three significant works resulting from Farmer's revision of the myth. Vividly written, *Lord Tyger* explores a fascinating theme: what a man raised under conditions approximating Tarzan's early life might actually become, particularly in mental outlook. The novel is both a first rate adventure and a visionary fable. Its premise has a mad South African millionaire, obsessed with the works of Burroughs, establishing a "controlled social experiment" in a remote valley of Ethiopia in order to show that a boy raised from infancy in the African wilderness would indeed grow up to be a primitive superman. Such an experiment is utterly inhuman, causing its subject and his parents enormous suffering. But the monomania of Boygur, the insane experimenter, is credible, for his fixation on Tarzan stems from his need to compensate for his own inferior body.

The novel is presented from the point of view of Ras Tyger, the subject of the experiment, as a young man coming of age in his Edenic habitat. Ras celebrates his innocent sensual life, then suffers a fall from innocence and searches for explanations of his existence, aided by a woman from the outside world. After many complications that test his mind and skills, Ras confronts his "creator," Boygur, passes judgment on him, and executes Boygur for tampering with his life. The story's melodramatic events are counterpointed by the inner drama of Ras's struggle to find the truth about his identity. In the creation of Ras's consciousness and in making his experience believable, Farmer has penned one of his major imaginative achievements.

Farmer first depicts Ras roaming his personal Eden, a young man totally in harmony with his natural environment, ruling beasts and fellow humans like some god of the jungle. Ras's foster parents, a pair of dwarfs pretending to be apes, can no longer control him in his young manhood. By strength and cunning, and by preying on their superstitions, Ras dominates a nearby tribe of blacks, as Tarzan did in *Tarzan of the Apes*. Ras also hunts leopards and other animals of the plateau, while enjoying a close friendship with a pet lion. Thus Ras's life approximates that of Burroughs' Tarzan, with minor variations. But Farmer provides Ras with a sexual education withheld from Burroughs' Tarzan, thanks to the black children of the Wantso village. Ras's sexual experimentation has been blissful and without the slightest trace of shame. He has explored oral and anal sex, tried casual homosexuality, and made love to a variety of black girls. As he has grown to manhood, he has also taken his pleasure with some of the wives in the black village.

However, Ras's sexual experience is innocent; lacking civilized inhibitions, he investigates sexuality in his puberty and adolescence with a freedom that hardly anyone with a civilized upbringing can ever hope to, even as a supposedly "liberated" adult. The opening scene shows Ras exulting in his prowess as he sings in a naively lyrical way of sexual joys:

O brown-skinned beauties, I love you. I love you as the lightning
its tall tree, the fish its water, the snake its hole in the ground.

Most of all, I love you, Wilida, because you are the most beautiful
and because you are guarded from me.

I, Lord Tyger, beautiful and fierce, leopard-beautiful, leopard
angry, Tyger, Tyger, from the Land of the Ghosts, ghost with the
long, long python between the thighs and the great beehives that
fountain forth honey on honey...."

Accompanying his song on a flute, Ras appears to be almost an elemental Pan, or (to use Nietzsche's concept), a Dionysian spirit of nature. In short, Farmer endows Ras with the kind of Rousseauist or unspoiled sexual nature that modern humanity is denied by civilization, yet dreams of possessing. To emphasize the point, significant mythic parallels are woven into the texture of the novel. Ras's foster parents are Mariyam and Yusufu, names which suggest Mary and Joseph and allusions to the story of Christ. Moreover, Mariyam tells Ras that Yusufu is only a foster father, and that his real father is God, or Igziyabher, a native name for God that suggests a parody of the biblical Yahweh. Like many mythic heroes, then, Ras grows up believing himself to be the son of a divine father, whom he associates with the top of a stone pillar from which Boygur directs the experiment. Since Boygur has planned Ras's life, and tries to control Ras's environment completely, there is an ironic truth in Ras's belief that he is the son of God. Finally, Ras's last name, Tyger, though the actual surname of the family from which he was kidnapped as a baby, also suggests an allusion to William Blake's poem, "Tyger, Tyger," celebrating an awesome and appalling force of nature.

Having created a sexually liberated and open Dionysian consciousness in Ras, Boygur, an imperfect and puritanical father "god," wishes to destroy it and end Ras's sexual freedom. To do so, he ends Ras's Edenic paradise of nature and sex by killing his foster mother. Trying to force Ras to follow the scenario of "The Book," *Tarzan of the Apes*, Boygur succeeds for a time. The innocent Ras turns into a vengeful killer who blames the Wantso for Mariyam's death and wages a lethal war against them to assuage his grief.

But Ras's fall from innocence continues when he meets his Eve, a blonde anthropologist on a field trip, appropriately named Eeva. The survivor of a plane crash that killed her husband, this worldly woman is not at all the innocent Jane whom Boygur wants Ras to find, but an experienced Finnish widow who makes Ras aware of the flaws in his Edenic existence.

Ras helps Eeva escape from Boygur's men and their helicopters and napalm—they wage war like General Westmoreland in Vietnam—and Eeva in turn helps Ras escape from the limited myths that shape his view of the world. Thus, in this fable Eve, or the feminine principle, does not bring sexual initiation, but an initiation into self-consciousness and the "knowledge of good and evil" according to the contemporary world. Ras's fall into moral awareness is symbolized by the river journey beyond the boundaries of his "happy valley." To emphasize the fall into self-consciousness that is occurring, Farmer at one point has Ras describe the river in serpent imagery: "'It's like a snake looking for a female in mating season,' Ras said." Thus the river journey plays the role of mythic snake to Eeva's Eve, as Ras's story becomes another version of "paradise lost."

The journey down river takes Ras and Eeva out of Ras's known territory, but not to the wise old man in a cave who will provide answers, as Ras's mythology had asserted. Wisdom is hard-earned in Farmer's world, and its beginning for Ras comes only with his escape from another black tribe, the Sharrikt, his acceptance of Eeva's view of the world, and his return to confront Boygur. Ras succeeds in his journey to moral maturity only because of his nature as a daring trickster and hunter. In the later sections of the book, two powerful scenes stand out: Ras's hunting of a crocodile and his seduction of Eeva with the still beating heart of the slain crocodile Not many writers would have the audacity to describe either scene.

In the novel's climactic sequence, Ras returns to his valley on the mesa and ascends the stone pillar to confront Boygur, his virtual creator and the would-be tyrant of his life. After destroying Boygur's mercenaries, Ras captures the insane Boygur in a noose and arraigns Boygur for his crimes. Boygur's transgressions include tampering with Ras's life and killing Mariyam; ruining the lives of Ras's older brothers, kidnapped earlier for failed experiments; and driving Ras's parents, an actual English lord and lady, to suicide from the loss of their children. Others were harmed to a lesser extent.

Implicit in Ras's confrontation of Boygur is an allegory of a Promethean and Dionysian hero confronting an insane and incompetent creator and calling him to judgment. Ras also symbolizes the archaic primitive psyche of pre-industrial man rejecting and overthrowing the rationalist, puritan god of a technological civilization, a god image inimical to the full humanity of mankind. As we have noted, father god figures nearly always turn out to be incompetent, egotistical, or completely insane in Farmer's work, and certainly inferior to the humans they are supposed to rule. Ras can free himself only by overthrowing Boygur, who is hurled from his pseudo heaven like Satan.

Lord Tyger comes to a calm resolution when Eeva takes charge of Ras's departure from Africa for civilization. The outside world comes into Boygur's valley, and Ras is flown with Eeva to America, where Eeva immediately begins to forget her love for him in the prosaic business of turning Ras's story into a commercial success. At first, Ras falls ill, his psychological trauma having been augmented by numerous inoculations. But soon he begins to recover in a New York hospital, and his chagrin at Eeva's neglect of him is relieved by the sexual attentions of a pair of nurses. Such feminine assistance helps Ras to accept the inevitability of his loss of paradise. He tells Eeva that "To be well in this civilization, you have to get very sick first. Just as, to be fully alive, you must first die." Farmer portrays Ras as quite prepared to pursue a career of lusty sexual enjoyment in the civilized world, which, despite its "dangers," also "had its compensating pleasure."

If *Lord Tyger* has any major fault, it is probably Farmer's ending: Ras's adjustment to civilization and a consciousness that combines desire and prudence may be portrayed as far too easy. The shock of moving from Ras's primitive life to modern culture might well produce a nervous breakdown. However, in Farmer's defense, Ras is consistently presented as a mentally resilient character, able to rebound quickly from any crisis.

In other respects, *Lord Tyger* is a rather impressive book. Farmer shows considerable erudition in his use of words from Amharic, and in his well-researched command of the Ethiopian setting. The reader becomes completely immersed in Ras's world, which is described in boldly visual and forceful imagery. But most important, perhaps, is Farmer's thoroughly convincing depiction of Ras's savage Dionysian consciousness. In describing Ras's innocent sexual education, for example, Farmer manages to convey his deepest social criticism as effectively as in his dystopia, *The Lovers*. *Lord Tyger* is probably Farmer's most satisfying evocation of the noble savage ideal and of innocent, uninhibited sexuality.

V

The Virtuoso Artist

(1)

Although some of Farmer's work is frankly conceived as entertaining adventure fiction, there is no denying the high level of craftsmanship in most of it. By 1969, when Farmer was finally able to write full time, he had transformed himself from the promising new talent of the fifties, full of energy and provocative ideas, but inexperienced, into a disciplined professional who would demonstrate his mastery in *Tarzan Alive* and the Riverworld novels. Some of the shortcomings of Farmer's more ambitious novels of the 1960s are probably due to the pressures under which they were written: the artist, regardless of his medium, needs time to contemplate his work and to shape his materials.

Farmer's potential had always been apparent to sensitive readers, especially in the shorter fiction. In the seventies, however, Farmer began to emerge as an artist of astonishing virtuosity. In addition to his Tarzan and Riverworld fiction, Farmer published sophisticated parodies of pulp thrillers, numerous "fictional author" stories, including the famous *Venus on the Half Shell*, and accomplished "experimental" or anti-realist "post-modernist" short fiction similar to that written by Robert Coover, John Barth, and Farmer's fellow Peorian, George Chambers. As we have noted, the "biography" of Lord Greystoke can be also seen as a fairly original experiment in fictional form. While acknowledging that Farmer's verbal artistry is an important advance in understanding his work, one should not neglect the social criticism and philosophic themes that continue to find a voice in it. If Farmer was once in danger of being taken as merely a prophet of the sexual revolution, there is a counter tendency now to read him only as an accomplished parodist and artistic technician. Both views are one-sided.

(2)

In the middle sixties, a new Farmer appeared with "Riders of the Purple Wage," a Joycean narrative written for Harlan Ellison's famous anthology *Dangerous Visions* (1967). This award-winning story explodes in a coruscating flash of puns and outrageous imagery, which seem both to imitate and parody *Finnegans Wake*. Yet the style is not verbal exhibitionism, but the perfect counterpart to the action described, the energetic searches of a puzzled youth in an anarchic, although supposedly beneficent, future society. The setting is the year 2166, in the Beverly Hills area of Southern California, where economic abundance has given everyone a high standard of living with little labor (a sixties conception that seems overly optimistic today). The "purple wage" of the title, besides parodying Zane Grey's "purple sage" (the dystopian future West rather than the romanticized Old West) refers to the food and other goods provided by a benevolent, government controlled economic system. Society is dominated and harassed by the media, constantly in search of novelty to ward off the universal enemy, boredom. "Fido," the advanced television of the day, is ubiquitous and soporific: millions watch it in place of finding meaningful activity: "their brains run to mud and their bodies to sludge." Pleasure and complacency are supplied by the "fornixcator," a machine that sends electrical jolts into the "fornix" area of the brain and produces orgasms: this is a satirical image of technologically efficient masturbation foreshadowing the pleasure machine in Woody Allen's brilliantly satiric film, *Sleeper* (1973).

Incongruously, Farmer's future society evinces both widespread erudition, thanks to "fido," and widespread barbarism—restless teenage gangs on the rampage as a mindless way of working off energies. Law-abiding citizens are encouraged to find self-fulfillment through various activities in the arts; unfortunately, such a solution does not work very well, for most lack either the talent or the will to be artistically successful.

Obviously, Farmer has created a lively satirical "anatomy," to use Northrop Frye's term, a comic and grotesque portrait of a disordered society. Farmer's dystopian world unfolds through a series of lively scenes and characters, mainly presented through Chib, a young artist undergoing a series of initiations, and Grandpa Winnegan, his great-great-grandfather, a persona representing Farmer himself. While Chib experiences the anomalies of his world, Grandpa Winnegan makes sardonic comments on them.

Winnegan, a hundred and twenty-year-old recluse, has cheated the government of taxes by keeping a private fortune, and is a fine comic creation. Both trickster and philosopher, embodying wily Ulysses and indestructible Finnegan archetypes, Winnegan represents one of the last exemplars of traditional individualism in the twenty-second century world. His aphorisms combine horrendous puns with incisive humanist social comment. Winnegan's death provides one of the story's best jokes: at his funeral there is a mock resurrection accompanied by the phrase "Winnegans Fake," a mocking pun on *Finnegans Wake*.

A satirical incident that has particular relevance to the science fiction genre involves an sf authoress, Huga Wells-Erb Heinsturbury, one of Chib's colleagues among the "Young Radishes," or radical artists. The name condenses references to six major figures in science fiction history: Hugo Gernsbach, H.G. Wells, Edgar Rice Burroughs, Robert Heinlein, Theodore Sturgeon, and Ray Bradbury. Huga attacks a *Time* newsman because of *Time*'s long-standing policy of sneering at science fiction. The humor in the incident cuts both ways, gently mocking both *Time* and the science fiction establishment.

An even more amusing irony in light of Huga's attack on the reporter is the fact that when *Time* finally began to notice science fiction, one of their first reviews was an approving, if mildly inaccurate, discussion of Farmer's fourth

Riverworld novel, *The Magic Labyrinth*. (Since this review appeared in the July 28, 1980, issue, some time after the success of *Star Wars* in 1977 and well after *Newsweek* discovered Ursula Le Guin and other science fiction novels, *Time* cannot be accused of acting hastily.)

"Riders of the Purple Wage" is a fine work, combining social criticism and experimentation in fictional form. This combination is also found in two other stories set in Beverly Hills, which together with "Riders" form what Farmer calls his Beverly Hills Trilogy. The second story in the Trilogy, "Down in the Black Gang" (first published in 1969; later rewritten for the anthology of the same title), abandons the ribald comedy of "Purple Wage" for a much grimmer tone. "Down" examines the dark side of Beverly Hills, the city that symbolizes wealth and the achievement of the American dream. The action is presented in the mode of traditional realism, but Farmer employs an innovative narrative point of view by making the narrator an alien, a member of the "black gang" (the phrase is from an old Bulldog Drummond title), and a traveler on a cosmic space ship fueled by raging human emotions. The narrator here functions as a symbol of impersonal forces in the unconscious part of the psyche, like the gods or daimons of Greek myth.

The narrator relates the story of two struggling families in a down-at-the-heels apartment house, and the tragedy that erupts when their frustrations finally become unbearable. One family, the Bonders, are Wasps who grapple with guilt over rebelling against their parents while they agonize over the future of the daughter and granddaughter who live with them. Much of Tom Bonder's frustration, however, results from thwarted professional ambitions; at forty-nine, he works as an electronic technician by day and labors over detective novels and westerns by night and on weekends. Obviously Bonder is a reflection of Farmer in the middle stage of his career.

The other family is the Fertigs, Jews beset by personal traumas and the spectre of failure. Mrs. Fertig is turning into an obsessive Jewish mother, both nagging and protecting her husband, while Myron Fertig, like Bonder a frustrated artist, cannot hold a job and is losing his ambition to be a cartoonist. The Fertigs are a Beverly Hills rarity, a family on food stamps and welfare, circumstances that double their humiliation; they also must suffer through the nights with an insomniac child.

This story of failed hopes reaches a crisis when Tom Bonder's frustration explodes into rage and an act of symbolic violence. Among other harassments, Bonder finds the crying of the Fertig child unbearable and races downstairs to the Fertig apartment with a hatchet, which he places inside the door and leaves. Though Bonder maintains control and finds release in a symbolic gesture, Myron Fertig is not so fortunate: he kills his wife and child with the axe, and then drives a butcher-knife into his own body. Bonder's guilt is thus doubled, for he has made himself accomplice to a horrifying crime.

This harsh tale is told with restraint and compassion. The compassion emerges both in the tone and in the narrator's final comments on the events. Rebelling against his role as a provoker of human emotion, the alien narrator, now humanized by his observation of a senseless tragedy, cries, "Somehow, there has to be a better way to run the Ship!" Those who doubt the seriousness of Farmer's concern over the human predicament, or his ability to deal with suffering and tragedy, should consider this story thoughtfully.

The third story of the trilogy is set in a different key. "Brass and Gold (Or

Horse and Zeppelin in Beverly Hills)'' was first published in *Quark*, a fine but short-lived anthology series of experimental science fiction; later it was reprinted in Farmer's 1979 collection, *Riverworld and Other Stories*. It is a comic but rather somber tale of a starcrossed love affair between two American dreamers, ''a drunken goy poet from Utah,'' a cowboy out of his time, and a frustrated Jewish wife, whose husband is obsessed with business. The tone of the story is light but restrained, unlike the pyrotechnic comedy of ''Purple Wage,'' and the action is fantastic and surrealistic, rather than realistic. Grotesque imagery prevails: Beverly Hills residents hang their money on clotheslines to dry; Mrs. Miteymans ''labored for twenty hours before giving birth to a thousand dollar bill''; imprisoned in her bedroom, Samantha Gold loses enough weight to squeeze under the door. Samantha's father, a German naval officer in 1918, builds replicas of his dirigible in his backyard in the ''poor section'' of Beverly Hills. Eventually the story seems to fade away when Samantha chooses eating pork over her love affair, her father flies off in a zeppelin, and Brass's horse dies on the pavement from pollution, forcing him to leave for the mountains of Utah.

In ''Brass and Gold'' Farmer moves directly into the mode of the anti-realist fiction of the sixties and seventies, as developed by Barth, Pynchon, Robert Coover (in his shorter fiction), and others. Beneath its surface lightness, the story reveals both melancholy and compassion. Its satire on American materialism and its obsession with technology is all the more effective because of its restraint.

(3)

In the middle seventies Farmer began a series of ''fictional author'' tales, stories by authors who have appeared as characters in fiction (for example, Paul Chapin and Harry Manders). These display his liberal talents for pastiche and parody. Probably the most important result of this enterprise, however, was the novel, *Venus on the Half-Shell*, which I discuss later. In the same period, Farmer wrote several parodies of pulp stories, the ''Greatheart Silver'' tales, for the anthology series *Weird Heroes*.

In this series Farmer condenses many pulp and literary allusions into the name of his hero, combining Mr. Greatheart from *Pilgrim's Progress*, Long John Silver, Max Brand's Silvertip, as well as just a hint of the Lone Ranger. Silver is classified as a truly American hero, descended from Thomas Jefferson by way of his black mistress, Sally Hemings, and also from the Sioux chief, Crazy Horse. All races are represented in his heritage. The Silver stories take place in a hallucinatory or dream American landscape that is vividly imagined. At times their humor is rather broad, and like all parody they run the danger of lapsing into triviality, but they show a lively imagination.

Another example of Farmer's mastery of parody is ''The Jungle Rot Kid on the Nod'' (1968), a brief story that presents Tarzan in the style of William Burroughs, rather than Edgar Rice. There is great vitality in this piece, an experiment with language (including many so-called obscene words) that becomes a collage of graphic images.

Whereas ''Jungle Rot Kid'' treats Tarzan in the language of earthy sexuality, an uninhibited sexual adventurer is portrayed through the imagery of World War I flyers and their exploits in the ribald ''Henry Miller Dawn Patrol'' (1977). In this comic lark, Henry Miller, a septuagenarian—a retired carpenter whose most exciting experiences came during his youth as a pilot in World War I—roams his nursing home looking for attractive elderly ladies with whom to gratify his persistent desires. Miller's early morning raids on willing female patients, some of them too sleepy to know what's happening, are described amusingly in metaphors of flight. What could have been a tasteless story becomes a delightful and gentle satire, reminding us that even the aged long for more intense sexual lives. The use of "Henry Miller" as a name for the main character also suggests another theme: the iconoclastic author, Henry Miller, is, whatever his literary faults, a good example of the writer who makes the celebration of sexuality a kind of protest against death and fear of oblivion which haunts all people; and Farmer's Henry Miller, the nursing home outlaw, is using sexuality to make his own protest against old age and dying. Appropriately, Miller dies as he expresses his defiance of the "Black Eagle" of death in a final epic copulation. This story provides evidence that Farmer's celebration of sexuality is rooted in a concern for fulfillment in life and a rebellion against death.

Perhaps the most outrageous parody or experimental story in Farmer's work is the recent "J.C. on the Dude Ranch" (1979), one of Farmer's funniest performances. Here Farmer uses the Christian archetypes of Christ and Satan in a mock heroic parody of Christian eschatology which also parodies the American western. Impressively handled, the language of the story is the Western vernacular of an old ranch hand, Soapy Waters, who relates a "tall tale" encounter between J.C. Marison and a Satan archetype. J.C. Marison ("Mary's Son") is a mysterious stranger at the XR Ranch, whose main distinguishing feature is not his guns, but phallus: "the crotch of his Levis seemed bigger'n a cow's udder. He was a natural for the XR." The black-hatted Satanic stranger also has impressive masculine credentials. While the black hat plans to foreclose the mortgage, J.C. demonstrates his prowess in seemingly miraculous ways, roping a runaway steer with a halo and turning three gallon jugs of water into hard liquor.

An apocalyptic mood is established by an evangelistic sheriff who has built the "Church of the Last Days," and who at first mistakes J.C. for the anti-Christ. But the sheriff identifies the true devil when he sees the black-hatted stranger fornicating with an insatiable female guest, Mrs. Lott; and learns that the devil not only has two horns, but two phalluses as well. The sheriff is rescued from the devil's wrath by J.C., who hogties Satan and carries him off. Everything fantastic in the story is then given a science fiction rationale, though the "reasonable" explanation of events seems just as fantastic as everything else.

"J.C. on the Dude Ranch" treats the archetypes of the Christian myth and the mythology of the western story in the spirit of Rabelaisian comedy. At the same time, the exuberant exaggeration of this parody seems to breathe some new life into traditional archetypes. Like the other short fiction I have discussed here, "J. C. on the Dude Ranch" is a story of considerable artistry. It appeared for the first time in *Riverworld and Other Stories* (1979), along with "Jungle Rot Kid," "The Henry Miller Dawn Patrol," and "Brass and Gold," among others. This collection demonstrates Farmer's disciplined imagination and vitality of language and shows his mastery of the anti-realistic "new fiction" techniques. Farmer's considerable talent for exuberant comedy and social satire is also confirmed by these stories.

Farmer's most important parody and fictional author story is *Venus on the Half-Shell* (1975), published by Dell books under the byline "Kilgore Trout." Trout is Vonnegut's itinerant, impoverished science fiction author, a prophet despised and without honor in his own country. A strong admirer of Vonnegut, Farmer has also confessed to a deep identification with Trout (who was actually suggested by Theodore Sturgeon). The identification was strengthened by many things: Farmer's own years as a struggling science fiction author in the early and middle stages of his career; Farmer's experience as a misunderstood social critic; and Farmer's identification with pornography as an Essex House author, a fate that plagued Trout. Finally, not long after Farmer had returned to Peoria, he was accused in 1970 of having written a letter signed "Trout" in the *Peoria Journal Star* criticizing President Nixon's Vietnam policy—another ironic identification of Farmer and Trout. (The letter is believed to have actually been penned by a college student.)

At any rate, Farmer, when afflicted with a temporary writer's block, conceived the idea of writing one of Trout's nonexistent novels and publishing it under Trout's name. He obtained Vonnegut's permission and went to work. When *Venus on the Half-Shell* was published by Dell, with Farmer wearing a false beard and a Confederate hat as a disguise on the back cover, the book was a ninety-day wonder, until Farmer's authorship, which Farmer made little effort to conceal, became known. Although the novel brought Farmer some unaccustomed notoriety (and made Vonnegut regret giving his permission to the project), the revelation of Farmer's authorship created a tendency to dismiss the work as simply an amusing parody and literary hoax. An additional irony in this episode has been Vonnegut's claim in a recent interview with Charles Platt (recorded in a book published in 1980) that Farmer failed to avow his authorship of *Venus* for a long period, presumably in the hope that sales would be increased by association with Vonnegut's reputation. This allegation, however, is not borne out by fact: Farmer told numerous friends, colleagues, and fans of his authorhip; in fact, he informed the present writer of it when *Venus* was appearing as a serial in *Fantasy and Science Fiction*. Vonnegut's reaction is perhaps not surprising, since Trout is his invention. But when Vonnegut professes to feel anxiety that Farmer's book may somehow have harmed his literary reputation, it is hard to take him seriously. Such concern might have been better devoted to the effect of Vonnegut's self-indulgent seventies novels, *Breakfast of Champions* and *Slapstick*.

Divorced from topicality and controversy, *Venus on the Half-Shell* can be read as a lively satirical anatomy, an absurdist novel that manages to parody Vonnegut while ridiculing human pretentiousness and our persistent search for metaphysical answers in an irrational universe. The novel makes effective use of lightness of tone and a casual treatment of catastrophe to present irreverent comments on the illusions of humans and the absurdity of events as this book presents them. One clue to the novel's theme is the hero's name, Simon Wagstaff, which evokes the tone of a Marx Brothers film.

Venus satirizes numerous ideals. The ethics of sexual conduct are spoofed by the descriptions of life among the Giffardians, sentient dirigibles. Teleological goals are satirized by such societies as the planet of thinking wheels, whose idea of the meaning of life is "getting there." The male fantasy of the perfect woman is parodied by the Venus of the novel, the android Chworktap, who has been programmed to be the perfect mate. (Nevertheless, she nags and makes tart comments.) The ideal of an eternal love is shown to be folly since, even though Simon has received immortality from a sexual interlude with an alien woman, and Chworktap has been built to endure for ages, they finally agree to part.

Farmer's theme of an absurd universe is developed in the final sequence, when Simon at last locates the first planet created and the galaxy's original species, one of whom is supposed to remember the Creator. The Clerun-Gowph, the first species, turn out to be gigantic, sentient cockroaches. Their oldest member grotesquely reveals that the universe was created by an idiot as a "scientific experiment," with this creator then wandering off and blanking out its memory. When Simon protests that such a creator showed an enormous indifference to suffering, the reply is, "Why not?"

Although this ending suggests that the universe may be absurd, it does not eliminate the possibility of meaning in life. Farmer satirizes the human tendency to seek meaning in revelations about the creator, rather than facing the fact that meaning must be created by humans themselves. Like other Farmer works, the novel presents the image of an incompetent or indifferent creator who abandons his creation to whatever ills beset it.

As a satire, *Venus on the Half-Shell* has many excellent moments, but it contrasts sharply with Vonnegut's work. Whereas Vonnegut is Juvenalian or Swiftian in his tone, his work suggesting genuine misanthropy, Farmer is a genial Horatian satirist here. There seems to be more readiness to accept the limitations of human life in Farmer, more hopefulness about the human capacity to enjoy life, even if dreams and ideals are for the most part doomed to not to be realized completely.

(5)

If Farmer has written a satire on the human condition in *Venus on the Half-Shell*, the same Farmer has also written a utopian novel called *Jesus on Mars* (1979). This book originated in a dream Farmer had of the title, but unlike Farmer's spirited parody in "J.C. on the Dude Ranch," *Jesus* is serious in tone, containing Farmer's most mature thought about the Christ of the gospels in the light of historical scholarship on the New Testament. But Farmer's novel is far more than a portrait of Jesus as Farmer conceives him: it is also a fable about the Second Coming of a messianic Jesus to earth, an event ushering in a millennial or utopian age. Whatever one finally thinks about Farmer's vision of Christ, it must be conceded that *Jesus on Mars* attempts to make imaginative use of the gospels on a more ambitious level than other science fiction treatments of the same subject (as in Ray Bradbury's story, "The Man," or Michael Moorcock's novel, *Behold the Man*).

The novel begins like a mundane and realistic space exploration story. Terrestrial explorers are preparing to land on Mars in 2015, during the first manned expedition to that planet. Mars, once the frontier of the imagination for Burroughs, C.S. Lewis, Leigh Brackett, Bradbury, and others, now seems like a visit next door. But Farmer sustains interest in the early stages by developing the characterizations of his quartet of space travelers. The group is meant to be a fairly international and representative assortment: Avram

Bronski, an agnostic French Jew of Polish antecedents; Nadir Shiraz, an Iranian-Scottish Muslim; Madeline Danton, the inevitable feminist, an agnostic French woman; and Richard Orme, a black Canadian Baptist who provides the novel's point of view. (Orme seems to be something of a fundamentalist, but a fairly reasonable one, until the end of the novel, when he finally caves in under internal pressures.) The use of a black protagonist is characteristic of a tendency among more liberal science fiction writers in the seventies, and of Farmer in particular, to draw on a wider range of ethnic types for major characters than science fiction used in the past.

After landing on Mars, the expedition experiences the shock of finding the planet inhabited, and the second stage of the plot begins as the explorers are introduced to a utopian civilization living undergound, at first glance behaving like orthodox Jews. The terrestrials enter the caverns to learn more about this world, another of Farmer's uses of an archetypal descent into the underworld. The utopian society is revealed as an intermarriage of humanoids called Krsh, the possessors of an advanced technology, and a community of Libyan Jewish Christians picked up from earth in the first century A.D. After both groups had settled on Mars, the Christians had converted the Krsh while accepting their science, thus providing their descendents with the best of both worlds. Since the Martian Christians are rather conservative, their community practices what Farmer conceives primitive Christianity to have been, a reformed Judaism with much traditional ritual, but a liberalized ethic of brotherhood and compassion.

A portrait of the historical Jesus before Greek and Roman Catholic patristic theology interpreted his life is presented through the gospel of Matthias, a "fifth gospel" that the Martian Christians accept as their supreme authority. In this book, showing Farmer's conception of the authentic historical Jesus, Jesus appears as a liberal humanitarian teacher who believed himself the messiah and proclaimed the coming end of the world. His mission had been the messianic one of bringing repentance, hope, and peace, but crucifixion had probably not been in his plans. After his death, his disciples have attempted to follow his teachings, with some adjustments for the failure of the world to end; but no doctrine interpreting the crucifixion in terms of salvation by atonement has been developed on Mars. In Farmer's view, the atonement doctrine is a later perversion of Christ; for the Martians, it is unnecessary for another reason.

Thus far Farmer's novel would hardly surprise most agnostics or enlightened believers, both of whom would probably be aware of such views of Jesus' life and teachings. But the action takes an unexpected direction when Farmer suddenly introduces a living Jesus, whose religion is a humanist synthesis of faith, Christian ethics, and a highly advanced technology. This Jesus, a living messiah of a technological and humanist millennium, is Farmer's most original conception.

The Martian society and its revelations, which shake Orme's faith while undermining the scepticism of the other terrestrials, is already affecting the characters when the new Jesus is introduced, initiating the third stage of the novel. The terrestrials learn that the Jesus of Matthias' gospel is said to be alive, living in a globe of gas suspended in the air inside a cavern. Periodically he makes visits to his followers and performs new miracles. The narrative now takes on the task of portraying Jesus himself when he descends, and describing his impact on the visitors from Earth.

Farmer depicts the living Jesus as an urbane and compassionate liberal, still dedicated to a messianic mission. Moreover, this Jesus performs authentic miracles as dramatic as any recounted in the gospels. On further acquaintance, Jesus is shown to be a genial spirit who drinks in moderation and has modified his earlier teachings about celibacy by taking a wife. It would be difficult to imagine Farmer protraying a messianic leader sympathetically unless the latter recognized his sexual nature and showed respect for the feminine principle, two of Farmer's dominant themes.) Nor is Jesus uncharitable toward sceptics: he faces Orme's doubts without concern, and shows a cosmopolitan tolerance for youthful rebels and dissenters. In fact, Jesus confides to Orme that certain questionable bars and cafes are actually maintained by the Martian state to serve as channels for the energies of youthful upstarts.

However, this Jesus, talking to Orme in hypothetical and ambiguous terms, reveals that his nature is natural, not supernatural, and that he is a self-created redeemer, rather than the spokesman for a transcendent creator. Jesus concedes that he is not the original Jesus of the gospels, the crucified human being, but an "energy being" who emigrated to Mars from another galaxy and assumed a human character modeled on the Jesus of Matthias's gospel. Thus Farmer, here as elsewhere in his work, transforms a supernatural myth to a naturalistic story using a science fiction rationale, although the transformed myth still holds numinous power.

Farmer's "energy being" is not only immortal, in his Jesus form, thanks to periodic visits to the globe of gas for self-renewal; he also has given himself a morally idealistic purpose in life. By becoming a humanist Jesus, he has assumed the role of a perfectionist spiritual leader. Successful with the Martian society developed from the union of Jewish Christians and Krsh, this Jesus now plans to take his gospel to earth in order to create a millennium of international peace and brotherhood.

Ironically, the terrestrial sceptics on the Mars expedition are converted, while Orme, the believer, harbors reservations. Orme's effort to thwart Jesus and the Martians in their mission to Earth provides the drama in the fourth and concluding section of the novel. Orme's doubts occur ostensibly because he fears that the shock of a living Jesus accompanied by the extraordinary Krsh science will throw twenty-first century Earth into turmoil. Nations and religious establishments will be threatened by the powerful figure of Jesus, and world-wide anarchy will result, Orme believes, from the clamor of individual citizens to share immediately in the benefits of Krsh science. Finally, Orme convinces himself that Jesus is a dangerous charlatan who will destroy individual liberty. But much of Orme's resistance to Jesus is based on an unconscious reaction caused by the phenomenon of a living savior (a disturbance of Orme's value system).

The novel's conclusion is visionary, and it may well be Farmer's most controversial ending. After informing Earth of their coming, Jesus and his Martian followers blast off to usher in a new golden age, taking Orme along. With apprehensive and sceptical national and religious leaders on hand to greet the messiah in the presence of television cameras, Orme tries to assassinate Jesus, but fails and is killed by security guards. Yet in a moment, Orme awakes, restored to life by a numinous Jesus in a triumphant miracle, the symbol of Jesus' forgiveness as well as his healing powers. The final irony is that Orme's attempt to thwart Jesus' mission has allowed Jesus to provide convincing proof of his powers. With Orme a reluctant convert, Jesus now sets out to make peace on Earth a reality, the ultimate trickster hero on a mission to redeem humanity from itself.

Farmer's Jesus is presented seriously, and the novel moves beyond the level of superficial incident to a visionary portrait of a naturalistic second coming of Christ. Farmer's theme is that a humanist Christ, allied with the extraordinary Krsh technology (especially their command of medical science), could usher in a millennial age. Of course, Farmer's humanist Jesus is a symbolic figure, representing the spirit of a liberalized Christianity, purged of what Farmer would consider sectarian bigotry, superstition, and unnecessary supernaturalism. With its synthesis of scholarship, scientific speculation, and liberal humanism, the novel is intended as a kind of tribute to Farmer's Christian Science mother, to whom the book is dedicated, although it is neither orthodox Christian Science nor orthodox mainstream Christianity.

It should be emphasized that Farmer's view of a liberal Christianity here is messianic and millennial, rather than apocalyptic, despite the usual association of the second coming of Christ with the theme of apocalypse. As such the novel belongs to a tradition of messianic fables in American science fiction that reaches back as far as A.E. Van Vogt's *Slan* (1941), and includes such works as Robert A. Heinlein's *Stranger in a Strange Land* (1961). Curiously, these books have not made much use of Christian themes or symbols. Farmer's fable is much closer to Christian tradition than these earlier messianic works, and its ethical awareness is a good deal more sophisticated. *Jesus on Mars* demonstrates that a speculative spirit and moral concern continue to influence the vision of Farmer, even in the period of his greatest technical mastery.

VI
The Fabulous Riverworld

(1)

Farmer's five novels in the Riverworld sequence represent the supreme project of Farmer's career. Certainly the material for the books has preoccupied Farmer for nearly thirty years; for, as we have seen, the original Riverworld novel, *I Owe for the Flesh* (also called *River of Eternity*), was composed in 1952 for the Shasta contest. After Shasta failed to publish it, it was set aside for over a decade while Farmer worked on other fiction, partly because the market for lengthy science fiction novels was not very strong in the fifties and early sixties. As Farmer has written elsewhere, Frederik Pohl, after reading the manuscript in 1964, advised Farmer that the Riverworld concept was too large to be encompassed in a single book, and encouraged him to develop a series. Pohl's shrewd advice may thus be credited with stimulating Farmer to transform his dense original work into an epic series of finely crafted novels. Pohl further advised Farmer to pen novelettes for Pohl's magazine, *Worlds of Tomorrow*, based on Riverworld material. Farmer published two stories there, "Day of the Great Shout" (January 1965) and "The Suicide Express" (March 1966), and the resurrection of the Riverworld began. Both novelettes were incorporated into *To Your Scattered Bodies Go* when it appeared in 1971, although a third tale, "Riverworld," published in *Worlds of Tomorrow* in January 1966, remains an independent story. After its publication in 1971, *To Your Scattered Bodies Go* won the Hugo award, and the Riverworld novel series was launched. *The Fabulous Riverboat* followed in 1971, but it was not until the second half of the decade that Farmer began the lengthy third and fourth volumes of the epic series. In fact, Farmer had intended to limit the basic sequence to a trilogy, but the third book proved to be a manuscript of 400,000 words, and he still felt some uncertainty about an ending. Of necessity, the "third volume" was split in two, with *The Dark Design* appearing in 1977 and *The Magic Labyrinth* in 1980. In addition, *The Magic Labyrinth* grew to 220,000 words in revision, forcing Farmer to cut the book prior to publication. One long excision, a passage of twenty-five pages or five chapters from the battle between Sam Clemens' and King John's ships, has been printed in a limited edition by The Ellis Press of Peoria, Illinois. Although the four major volumes of the Riverworld series appeared to stand as a basic unit, Farmer was dissatisfied with *The Magic Labyrinth* as a resolution, and published *Gods of Riverworld* in the fall of 1983. Other volumes may appear, both in the main channel of the series, and on "sidestream" stories.

As we review the publishing history of the Riverworld novels, it becomes clear that Farmer's initial misfortune with the original Riverworld novel may have been a stroke of good luck, however frustrating it was at first. By the time he returned to the Riverworld material, he was more experienced as a writer; the novels published in the seventies show a mastery of the novel form surpassing even the best of the early novels, *The Lovers*. Moreover, the Riverworld concept is more effectively developed in a series than in an individual novel, if for no other reason than the use of multiple protagonists. Finally, the presentation of the Riverworld epic in a series enabled Farmer to build a considerable following for it by the time *The Magic Labyrinth* appeared. Thus, Farmer's industry and imagination eventually turned the disheartening circumstances of his early career into a stunning triumph.

(2)

The setting for the Riverworld stories is a planet whose dominant feature is a gigantic serpentine river winding between mountains and bluffs from polar sea to polar sea. At times the river widens to form lakes. Between mountains and river there are usually stretches of prairie or savannah, where all of humanity who have ever lived on Earth before 1983 (except for those aged five or under when they died), dwell in resurrected bodies. These thirty-six billion humans are resurrected in naked, twenty-five year old bodies, the men with no facial hair (Farmer dislikes beards, yet hates to shave). Although the setting suggests the dominance of nature, it is a nature ordered by a vast technology: the most basic human need, hunger, is supplied by food that appears in "grails" or metal containers, which also supply limited amounts of alcohol and tobacco. In the first two novels, when someone dies or is killed, he is mysteriously brought to life again somewhere else on the great river.

Obviously, the Riverworld is a "controlled social experiment" on an unprecedented scale, and the attempt to discover the reality behind the appearance provides much of the dramatic conflict in the novels. At this point, however, the question of sources deserves some attention. Where, besides his own imagination, did Farmer find the inspiration for this vast conception? Clearly Farmer had the Riverworld idea in mind long before actually writing the original novel (in a month).

Farmer himself offers two literary sources, neither of them from science fiction. One is *Huckleberry Finn*, with its seemingly endless journey down a river, and its symbolic overtones of the journey as a metaphor for life and the search for meaning, or simply the quest for the Great Good Place. A second source Farmer has cited in oral statements is *A House-Boat on the Styx*, by John Kendrick Bangs, which Farmer read in his youth. Published by Harper and Bros. in 1895, the book is a series of satirical dialogues between the famous dead dwelling in a houseboat moored on the river Styx in Hades. Among those who appear are Shakespeare, Sir Francis Bacon, Sir Walter Raleigh, Dr. Samuel Johnson, Nero, and Queen Elizabeth I. The dialogues are rather static, like the houseboat, but they treat satirically such literary and social topics of the day as feminism and whether Bacon wrote Shakespeare's plays. The author, John Kendrick Bangs, was a highbrow humorist who sometimes published in *Harper's Magazine*. A sequel, *The Pursuit of the House-Boat*, featured Sherlock Holmes in an attempt to capitalize on Holmes' fame after Doyle had supposedly killed him off, evidence that Bangs did not restrict himself to merely historical figures.

A reprint of *A House-Boat on the Styx* was published in 1973 by the Lost Cause Press at Louisville, Kentucky, and is readily available through the interlibrary loan system. But a perusal of Bangs' book does not show a very close kinship between it and the Riverworld novels: for instance, there is little or no narrative suspense or movement in Bangs' work, which can hardly be called a novel. The main similarity between Bangs and Farmer is the fact that both resurrect historical figures in order to make comments on human experience. However, another point is worth noting here. Immediately behind Bangs' dialogues is the tradition of the "imaginary conversation" or "dialogues of the dead," practiced by such nineteenth century authors as Walter Savage Landor. Even more important is the fact that Bangs' dialogues derive from classical mythology's "underworld" or land of the dead, even through this mythology is merely a literary convention, not a deeply felt imaginative concept, for Bangs. *A House-Boat on the Styx* thus provides a link between Farmer's work and the Greco-Roman legends of a Hades to which heroes make archetypal descents to test their courage and discover arcane truths.

In addition to literary sources for the Riverworld, the influence of a natural feature from the landscape of Farmer's childhood and youth should be mentioned. Anyone growing up in Peoria, Illinois, could hardly fail to be impressed with the most striking manifestation of nature in this environment: the Illinois River. Flowing through a rolling landscape of prairies and cornfields, the Illinois cuts a wide swath between deep bluffs, flanked by rugged ravines. The river often resembles Farmer's mythic River, sometimes widening to make lakes, sometimes twisting and snaking between narrow ramparts. Although the Illinois River is not quite the Mississippi, it is no trivial stream; in fact, it is the one natural feature in the Central Illinois landscape most likely to become a mythic force in the imagination.

Hence, both literary sources and environment probably helped this creation of the Riverworld. Allied with these sources, however, there is the archetypal theme of descent to the underworld and the journey through it by water, a theme celebrated in myth from Greek literature to the thought of C. G. Jung. Another obvious symbol of the resurrection of the body, which has a deep appeal for Farmer, although as usual with Farmer's treatment of Christian mythology, it is reinterpreted in a naturalistic rather than a supernatural form.

(3)

The independent novelette "Riverworld" is an overture to the series. Dissatisfied with the 1966 magazine version of 12,000 words (which had been reprinted in *Down in the Black Gang and Other Stories*, 1971), Farmer rewrote the story for his 1979 collection, *Riverworld and Other Stories*, expanding it to nearly 34,000 words. This revision, typical of the conscientious artistry of Farmer in the seventies, improves the characterizations of the tale considerably, and eliminates some details about Tom Mix's life which recent research has shown to be inaccurate.

The main characters are Mix and a resurrected Jewish prophet, Yeshua, to whom Mix bears an interesting facial resemblance, and who turns out, not very surprisingly, to be Farmer's first concept of the historical Jesus (years before *Jesus on Mars*). Mix and Yeshua represent opposed reactions to the Riverworld, Mix accepting his new life with heroic pragmatism, while Yeshua laments the inaccuracy of his theology, and feels anguish over the general hedonism and bitter sectarian conflicts around him. Both Yeshua and a woman named Bithniah are used to correct what Farmer considers to be the Bible's errors and distortions of history. Bithniah, a Hebrew woman from the time of Moses, offers Farmer's speculations on the book of *Exodus*: Moses probably had an Egyptian father; he was adopted by an Egyptian priest who practiced the forbidden monotheism of Aton, founded by the disgraced Pharoah Akhnaton; and experienced troubles because of his womanizing, before returning from Midian with his religion of Yahweh. Similarly, Yeshua offers some plausible "corrections" about the ministry of Jesus.

Mix shows curiosity but scepticism toward questions of religious truth and belief. His own philosophy is one of humane tolerance and stoic acceptance of whatever world he is in. He tries to bring Yeshua to his point of view:

> "Things can't be that bad," he said. "Maybe this world didn't turn out to be what you thought it was going to be. So what? You can't blame yourself for being wrong. Who could possibly have guessed the truth about the unguessable? Anyway, this world has many good things that Earth didn't have. Enjoy them. It's true it's not always a picnic here, but when was it on Earth? At least, you don't have to worry about growing old, there are plenty of good-looking women, you don't have to sit up nights wondering where your next meal is coming from or how you're going to pay your taxes or alimony. Hell, even if there aren't any horses or cars or movies here, I'll take this world anytime! You lose one thing; you gain another."

Yeshua, however, the permanent archetype of the moralist and aspiring spirit, is not persuaded by Mix, the embodiment of the tolerant man of the world.

Unfortunately, many of those in the Riverworld do not share Mix's tolerance. Mix and Yeshua are embroiled in a war between the state where they reside, ruled by William Stafford, a seventeenth-century English puritan zealot, and the theocracy of Kramer, a German Reformation fanatic. Stafford's little commonwealth is tolerable because Stafford, a moderately reasonable man, has modified his beliefs after the resurrection gave him cause to doubt the Bible. But Kramer, a domineering bigot, is the dictator of a monolithic state that represses dissent and wages war on countries which reject Kramer's dogmas. When Stafford's country is overrun, Mix and Yeshua are sentenced to be burned as heretics.

The irony is obvious enough: in the name of Christianity Jesus is burned because he is not a good Christian. The novelette ends with Yeshua's bitter ironic lament: "Father, they *do* know what they're doing!" This revision of the New Testament statement on the cross is appropriate because Kramer has chosen to disregard Yeshua's own testimony about his former life. Nor is the irony lessened much by the consolation that the heretics will be resurrected down river, for they still must suffer pain and humiliation.

"Riverworld" is a forceful tale, and Farmer's most explicit attack on Christian bigotry. While much of Farmer's work satirizes or criticizes puritanism and religious intolerance, "Riverworld" and the novels that follow assault the historicity of the Bible directly, and frequently—although not exclusively—identify fanaticism with a specific contemporary faith, Christianity. However, while this criticism of Christian intolerance is only a minor theme in the Riverworld novels it is almost the whole point of "Riverworld." The story displays a satirical and polemical spirit reminiscent of Voltaire, or the Twain of *The Mysterious Stranger*; but it is a work of fiction, not a polemic. Its characterizations of Yeshua and Mix are effective. Both are credible persons, not merely mouthpieces for Farmer's views. As opposed types of the mystic and the man of the world, they offer sensible alternatives to fanaticism. Farmer's sympathies for Mix's brand of stoic and realistic, if not very intellectual, humanism seem obvious here; but in the third and fourth Riverworld novels, Mix's views seem less impressive beside the determination of Farmer's more ambitious seekers for answers.

(4)

To Your Scattered Bodies Go introduces Richard Burton as a quest hero of Farmer's epic, and unveils the Riverworld universe more completely, while establishing as a theme the quest to solve the mystery of its origin. This novel enlarges the realm of experience Farmer has treated in fiction and contains some strong writing.

Farmer's Burton is a fairly convinceing character, effectively modeled on the historical Burton. It is to Farmer's advantage, of course, that while Sir Richard Burton is a literary legend, there is no well-defined personality of Burton in the public mind, for it could have been a difficult standard with which to compete. Farmer's command of the details of Burton's life and his identification with Burton provide him with good source material on which to base his characterization. Burton's tireless energy, wide experience with a variety of cultures, and considerable erudition give him the liberal and inquiring consciousness that Farmer needs for his major point of view in the narrative. In fact, before portraying Burton, Farmer had created perhaps only two protagonists, Carmody and Grandpa Winnegan, who reflected the scope and richness of Farmer's own mind. Moreover, Burton's array of physical talents and skills, which with his wide-ranging mind make him seem an Elizabethan who had strayed into the nineteenth century, are necessary heroic qualities for the challenges he will face.

Moreover, it is imaginatively appropriate for Burton to take on the task of searching for the source of the River: a man like Burton would be unlikely to settle down to comfortable mediocrity on the Riverbank. But the chance to search for the River's origin and learn the truth about the mysterious masters of his world gives Burton a perfect opportunity to redeem the major failures of his life. The historical Burton was caught up in the almost mystic fervor of nineteenth-century exploration: his great ambition was to find the source of the Nile, a quest that may have unconsciously symbolized a search for the origin of life or the meaning of existence for Burton and other Victorians. But though Burton came close to his goal, he failed through carelessness and bad luck. Burton's expedition did find Lake Tanganyika, which Burton mistakenly took to be the true source of the Nile. Since Burton's later life was always blighted by the shadow of this failure, his quest for the source of the river allows him his second chance. One of Farmer's central themes in the Riverworld novels is the human longing for a supreme wish fulfillment: the ability to rectify or obliterate the greatest mistake of one's former life. This motif is a theme of Shakespeare's later romances, appearing in such forms as Leontes receiving his wife's forgiveness and love after having apparently destroyed her by his angry jealousy. Burton's dream of redeeming his failure makes him an excellent choice for the role of seeker for the source of life and for meaning. Despite his considerable abilities, Burton is neither a superman nor without faults. Constantly angry with the conditions of his existence, Burton is frequently impatient and callous toward others. But his faults make him more sympathetic and easier for the reader to identify with; they serve to humanize his character and make it credible.

With one exception, the secondary characters in *To Your Scattered Bodies Go* are less memorable. Peter Jairus Frigate is a rather pale Farmer persona; Monat the Arcturan seems little different from the terrestrials; and Lev Ruach seems to be an obligatory Jewish character inserted to comment on Nazism and anti-Semitism. It comes as no shock to learn in *The Dark Design* that they are all agents of the Ethicals masquerading as resurrected humans. Alice Hargreaves, however, is a satisfactorily conceived heroine. Her gradual shedding of Victorian propieties and her sexual liberation under Burton's guidance are presented believably and tactfully. Alice's presence also has a stabilizing effect on Burton, as though his restless spirit requires an innocent Jungian *anima* figure to complement it. As always in Farmer's work, the hero's character is not whole or complete until it recognizes the feminine principle.

Vivid scenes of hallucinatory power dominate *To Your Scattered Bodies Go*. Burton's memories of his death, his awakening in the resurrection bubble, and the awe-inducing spectacle of resurrection morning are all depicted with visionary force. Burton's grim pursuit of his quest, including his willingness to die and be reborn 777 times, is effectively described. These repeated deaths and rebirths function well as symbols of the abasement and surrender of the ego in the face of an overwhelming purpose. Finally, Burton's encounters with the Ethicals have a properly surrealist quality.

The ending of the novel is impressive. Burton's quotation of Satan's lines from *Job* on his return from his journeys carries the resonance of conviction. At this point, Burton does become identified with the figure of Satan or Prometheus as an opponent of the gods and a critic of the mediocrity of humanity.

"Where have you been?" Frigate said.

"From going to and fro in the earth, and from walking up and down in it," Burton said. "However, unlike Satan, I found at least several perfect and upright men, fearing God and eschewing evil. Damn few, though. Most men and women are still the selfish, ignorant, superstitous, self-blinding hypocritical, cowardly wretches they were on earth. And in most, the red-eyed killer ape struggles with its keeper, society, and would break out and bloody its hands."

Burton's comments remind us of a secondary theme in the novel, which complements Burton's indomitable will to discover the truth about the Riverworld: Farmer's realistic assessment that most of humanity will waste their second chance at existence by failure to liberate themselves from blinding illusions. The readiness of most Riverworld dwellers to lapse into past superstitions and habits, or to settle for lives of inglorious mediocrity, provides a sharply ironic contrast to Burton's unswerving determination to reach the source of the River.

Burton's conflict with the self-styled Ethicals is also presented memorably. The Ethicals are portrayed as mysterious, ambiguous, and vaguely sinister. Although they seem to have godlike powers, they are clearly not perfect divinities, and their insistence on mystery in their attempts to control the Riverworld people as part of a vast experiment are clearly dubious from a moral point of view. As might be expected, beings who call themselves "Ethicals" are likely to be anything but ethical, and the name takes on ironic overtones by the end of the tale. Burton's struggle against the Ethicals presents in definitive form a characteristic theme in earlier Farmer novels: the conflict between a Farmer hero and the "gods" who would rule his world. Burton's secret relationship with the Ethical who betrays his fellows also links Burton and the mysterious X with the romantic archetype of the Satanic or Promethean rebel who opposes the gods, an identity Burton himself chooses deliberately.

To Your Scattered Bodies Go begins the Riverworld epic in a key of high drama. It is a haunting book—many of its scenes linger in the imagination. Such sustained visionary power is not found often enough in Farmer's earlier fiction. Leslie Fiedler lauded the first two Riverworld books by saying: "It is the deepest level of childhood response which Farmer has reached in this pair of novels." *To Your Scattered Bodies Go* earns such praise.

(5)

The Fabulous Riverboat, written not long after its predecessor, does not quite sustain the high dramatic level of *Scattered Bodies*, nor is the writing as vivid. Of course, Farmer could hardly repeat the memorable beginning of the first book, with the resurrection bubble experience followed by resurrection morning. Nevertheless, there are numerous similarities between the two books. But these are offset by Farmer's choice of Sam Clemens for a hero. Clemens is not only vastly different from Burton, but his characterization presents more formidable challenges.

This time Farmer has a character who, unlike Burton, is part of American folklore; and the problem is complicated by the contradiction between the affable public Mark Twain and the acerbic private Samuel Clemens, afflicted in his last years not only by misanthropy but by bitter despair and a sense of life's absurdity. The characterization of Clemens involves grave risks, despite Farmer's own feeling of identification with Clemens as a Midwestern iconoclast. Yet Farmer has some success with the character, partly by softening the extreme bitterness of Clemens' last years and making his Clemens a gruff and sardonic observer of human follies and pretentiousness, more like the Clemens of the middle years. Moreover, Farmer can portray Clemens as discovering new enthusiasm for existence, thanks to his unexpected resurrection. Clemens is given a satisfactory stock of Midwestern and Western phrases to express his frequently sulphurous comments. However, although Farmer can give Clemens some wit by allowing him to quote from his writing—and the novel might benefit from more of this—Farmer is not able to provide Clemens with enough original witticisms, of the sort that the historical Clemens might be expected to coin if resurrected in such circumstances. In short, the characterization of Clemens is plausible to some degree, but never quite as satisfactory as could be wished.

When the limitations of the Clemens characterization are acknowledged, they still allow him to be accepted on his own merits. Despite some faults, *The Fabulous Riverboat* is a spirited narrative, filled with trenchant comments on human experience. Clemens is surrounded by a group of well drawn characters including Firebrass, Joe Miller, and Cyrano de Bergerac, who is especially lively and engaging. There is much social comedy and outright irony. Clemens' rejection by his earthly wife, Livy, is an ironic reversal of Burton's affair with Alice in *To Your Scattered Bodies Go.* Nevertheless, Clemens gets himself enthusiastically involved in building the perfect riverboat and setting up his ideal state, Parolando. But while the "Mysterious Stranger" has given Clemens a quest akin to Burton's, it is obvious that Clemens is a different type from Burton, far more interested in the journey than the end of the quest, and more concerned with the building of the riverboat and founding his perfect state than with anything he might find at the Dark Tower in the polar sea. Like Burton, Clemens has some failures to redeem, but his vacillation and his proclivity to be distracted by the human comedy make him a rather ironic quest hero.

The major conflict of the book emerges in Clemens's association with King John, another effective characterization. John is a political trickster, a master of deceit who may be an ironic reflection of the age of Richard Nixon. The alliance with John becomes a test of Clemens's character and a revelation of his divided nature. Torn between feelings of generosity and tolerance toward fellow humans, and scepticism about their motives arising from his own dark knowledge of human behavior, Clemens embodies the dilemma of the political liberal. His instincts and his knowledge of history tell him not to trust John, a pragmatic opportunist who can be expected to break any agreement when betrayal becomes advantageous. But Clemens' desire to give humanity a second chance and his hope that even John can transcend past behavior, impel him to honor a disastrous alliance. Clemens' vacillations between his two natures are exasperating, although they make his character all the more believable. Predictably enough, Clemens is outraged by the treachery he halfway expects, and revenge becomes his dominating passion by the end of the novel, though such a reaction is as illogical as his decision to trust John.

There is room to doubt that the historical Clemens would have been so foolish as to expect John to honor an agreement or to treat the alliance as a test for his theories about humanity. Yet the historical Clemens was certainly guilty of atrocious judgment. If we forget reservations based on knowledge of the historical Clemens, Farmer's character is a complex and successful character, whose desire to trust humanity contradicts his disillusioned realism, and whose divided nature thus dramatizes the dilemmas that thoughtful liberals often confront.

Although *The Fabulous Riverboat* lacks the drama and the visionary force of its predecessor and seems in many ways an ironic parallel to the first book, Clemens's encounters with the mysterious stranger have some of the hallucinatory vividness of *To Your Scattered Bodies Go.* Social comedy and satire still play a large role in the novel, but the conflict between Clemens and John has the potential for tragedy, a theme fully developed in the fourth volume of the series.

(6)

Before beginning the final two Riverworld novels in the middle seventies, Farmer, according to his own testimony, sat down and re-read the first two: the result was that he found an "appalling" number of problems to be resolved and rational explanations to be devised. Such a reaction to the continuation of the series may seem a bit surprising: clearly, Farmer had a general scheme for completing the basic books of his epic. However, every strand of plot was not thoroughly worked out before Farmer began publishing, unlike the composition of a comparable epic, J.R.R. Tolkein's *The Lord of the Rings*. The Tolkien trilogy was submitted to a publisher as a whole after Tolkien had exhaustively developed the complications of his narrative and had laid out nearly every detail of the history, language, and culture of Middle Earth that concerned his story. By contrast, the Riverworld evolved as Farmer published his novels.

Farmer's concern with the resolution of problems raised in the first two books helps to explain some revelations made in *The Dark Design*. If these sometimes seem a little ingenious, they usually enhance credibility. For instance, it is now revealed that every person who supposedly lived after 1983 is actually an agent of the Ethicals. This is not merely a plot device to increase intrigue, but a way of protecting the novel from becoming dated, for nearly anything Farmer postulated about the history of the earth beyond 1983 would be inevitably disproven by events, and quite quickly for the two decades immediately following. This same revelation exposes the Frigate of the first novel as bogus, an agent who had assumed the identity of the genuine Frigate, partly to keep track of Burton. Thus Farmer eliminates the improbability of the true Frigate being resurrected near the idol of his earthly life.

The Dark Design ambitiously employs the device of multiple narratives, continuing the stories of Burton and Clemens, while adding those of the true Frigate and Jill Gulbirra. Though describing several searches for the dark tower, some thirty odd years after the Resurrection, the novel focuses on a quest that fails, the journey of the airship *Parseval* on which Jill is an officer.

The characterizations of *The Dark Design* are realistic and complex. Perhaps the most satisfying portrait is that of Gulbirra, the feminist airship pilot. Her characterization convincingly breaks with the traditional stereotypes of women in science fiction, and atones in part for the tendency of male writers to make the heroines of romance beautiful and bent on marriage. Gulbirra is not pretty by conventional standards, being flat-chested and buck-toothed. She is not only an ambitious woman pursuing a traditionally masculine career, but descended from a despised ethnic group, the Australian aborigines, which gives her the additional burden of being taken for a black (technically aborigines are Caucasians, but they have been given social roles similar to those inflicted on American blacks). Two emotions dominate Gulbirra, anger at the unequal treatment of women in social and professional circumstances, and pride in her own competence as an airship pilot. Bitterness against male chauvinism has driven Gulbirra to become bisexual, although, as Farmer portrays her, she does not find complete satisfaction in her relationships with either women or men. Gulbirra is one of Farmer's most original characters.

Other effective characterizations in *The Dark Design* include Piscator and the authentic Peter Jairus Frigate. Piscator, the Japanese mystic and fisherman, is one of the few colleagues to show sympathy for Gulbirra. A practicing Sufi, Piscator reflects, for the first time in Farmer's work, the influence of Sufi mysticism on the author. Farmer became interested in Sufism through his study of Burton, although Burton remarks in *The Magic Labyrinth* that all the Sufis he knew in Damascus were scoundrels. Although Farmer does not naively consider all Sufis to be of the stature of the saintly Piscator, he has publicly expressed interest in the Sufi tradition and has read widely in Sufi literature. The impact of Farmer's reading of Idries Shah and other writers on Sufism is shown not only in Farmer's characterization of the moderate and self-disciplined Piscator, but in the presence of numerous Sufi jokes in *The Dark Design*. Piscator's mystic quest is treated with complete sympathy. Farmer, of course, had treated mystical search with sympathetic characterization before, notably in Carmody and Yeshua. But both had been seen as following questionable revelations, whereas Piscator's Sufism is itself viewed with respect.

Farmer's characterization of the actual Frigate in *The Dark Design* is also complex and three-dimensional, in contrast to the sketchy treatment of the false Frigate in *To Your Scattered Bodies Go*. Farmer explores Frigate's inner life through his dreams and memories of boyhood and youth in Peoria. Frigate's human existence becomes more understandable and poignant as a result. *The Dark Design* is clearly the most autobiographical of Farmer's works. Farmer's introspective treatment of character is not limited to Gulbirra and Frigate, however. Clemens and Burton are also depicted through their inner lives of dream and memory. In many respects, *The Dark Design* is the most contemplative novel that Farmer has written, and for that reason, as well as for its realism and humor, can be rated very highly.

Literary allusions enrich the quest motifs in *The Dark Design*. Gulbirra's airship is named the *Parseval*, evoking overtones of the mythic quest for the holy grail, a motif already established in *To Your Scattered Bodies Go*. The search for the grail is alluded to jauntily, as is the Celtic motif of the quest for the "Undying Lands." Alice provides additional literary allusion by quoting Robert Browning's "Childe Roland to the Dark Tower Came," the poem celebrating the quixotic triumph of a flawed quest hero—an allusion particularly relevant to Burton. Finally, Piscator's name evokes the suggestion of a "fisher-king" figure from grail legend, a motif developed further when Piscator turns out to be dead, but is restored to life when Burton's party enters the tower and Alice manages to alter the computer's programming to restore fertility to the land. Farmer's use of the "fisher-king" motif plays loosely with the traditional version of the myth, but it reinforces the grail symbolism identified with the Dark Tower.

Although *The Dark Design* is an introspective novel, punctuated heavily with interludes of ribald humor, the final fourth of it rises to dramatic urgency. Farmer has gradually revealed that the quest for the Dark Tower involves more than a personal challenge for Burton or Clemens. There are hints that the Riverworld is merely an experiment that will be terminated when the Ethicals have gathered enough data, a situation that threatens the extinction of thirty-six billion people. Moreover, resurrections from death have ceased along the river, restoring death to its ancient role as king of terrors, and suggesting either that the Riverworld's technology is running down or that the experiment is gradually being dismantled.

Against this ominous background, *The Dark Design* concludes with the destruction of the *Parseval* before the Dark Tower can be explored. The Riverworld and the mysterious Ethicals remain an enigma, the novel's title hinting ambiguously at a pattern that contains little hope for humanity. Farmer's third novel in the series enlarges the stature of his characterizations and expands the search for the Dark Tower to added dimensions: the quest is no longer a personal obsession of Burton or Clemens, but one fraught with social significance. The mystic overtones of a search for meaning are also intensified.

(7)

The Magic Labyrinth, the fourth volume of the basic Riverworld saga, was the product of considerable rewriting on Farmer's part—especially the ending, for which, at one time, Farmer experimented with five variations. The novel abandons the contemplative and introspective mode of *The Dark Design* for a tense and concentrated narrative focused on dramatic action. Though introducing new minor characters, Farmer resists the tendency to digress. Two conflicts, Clemens's struggle with King John and Burton's expedition to the tower, are kept at center stage.

The decision to maintain a tight narrative focus obliged Farmer to make numerous excisions in his long manuscript version of 220,000 words. A major deletion referred to earlier describes the fate of Tom Mix and Jack London in the climactic battle between Clemens and John. Such an alteration reduces the status of Mix and London to minor roles. Another character who suffers from the tight narrative is Frigate, who is demoted, disappointingly, to a secondary status in *The Labyrinth* after being a major figure in *The Dark Design*.

Some characters do benefit from their treatment in *The Labyrinth*. The most obvious example is Herman Goring, the former Luftwaffe commander, who is presented as a complex individual. In Farmer's view, Goring was a flawed idealist and aristocrat who became involved with psychotic Nazis, and then truly repented after the fall of Germany. In the Riverworld, Goring has become almost saintly under the influence of the Church of the Second Chance, as he seeks to expiate his crimes by performing humanitarian acts. However, Goring cannot completely eradicate his past or escape feelings of violence reminiscent of his older self. He is drawn subtly, a portrait representing Farmer's art at its full maturity.

Two minor characters of note are Jacques Gillot, or La Viro, the founder of the Church of the Second Chance, and Blessed Croomes, a Southern black woman from the eighteenth century who fluctuates between hedonism and religious intensity. Gillot, the religious leader, is a compound of humility, mysticism, and reason; and his church, which attempts to deal realistically with the conditions of the Riverworld, is treated sympathetically as a kind of enlightened religious humanism comparable to the Christian society of *Jesus on Mars*. Croomes, who accompanies Burton in his climactic expedition, is another strong feminine characterization whose irrepressible nature helps her steal a scene or two.

The central thematic actions of the novel—the Riverworld war and Burton's expedition—are presented in thorough detail. Both Clemens and Burton are given important moments of dramatic introspection, Clemens in a long and surrealistic dream sequence and Burton in a vigorous soliloquy that recalls the Elizabethan drama. Each passage serves to pull together varied strands in the character's life to focus on the challenges he faces.

Farmer depicts Clemens's showdown with King John in the Riverworld war as shockingly violent and destructive. Despite the presence of the two grand riverboats and four World War I fighter pilots, which might seem to contribute a nostalgic aura to the battle, the combat uses efficient, sophisticated weapons and results in appalling carnage. In earlier books, Farmer had run the risk of seeming to romanticize violence, particularly when it occurred in such remote, quasi-fantasy settings as the "World of Tiers" or ancient Opar. The Riverworld war, however, is depicted with grim realism. By his harsh, anti-romantic description of the Riverworld war, Farmer shows that he can treat war convincingly in the manner of such novelists as Ernest Hemingway and Norman Mailer. Such a portrayal of combat stripped of its pretensions and glamor is a kind of definitive anti-war statement by Farmer which should clear up any misunderstanding of his attitude about war. The credibility of the imagined battles is all the more impressive because the author has not experienced war at first hand.

One exception to the anti-romantic tone of the war should be noted. This is is the duel between Burton and Cyrano de Bergerac. In an inferno of destruction the two meet in the manner of romantic tradition and stage an old-fashioned sword fight. Their actions are all the more remarkable because neither is intense about the outcome of the larger conflict, and because they treat each other with scrupulous respect and fairness. Their gentlemanly and chivalrous fight contrasts ironically with the barbarism of the Riverworld Armageddon. The duel also illustrates Farmer's contention that the individual can always manage to conduct himself with integrity and style, despite whatever social madness is raging.

The Riverworld war establishes Clemens as a tragic hero. The terrible destruction of the battle shows what was already obvious: lust for revenge on John distorts his character and threatens the peace and well-being of those on both ships. Where violence has wrought such wholesale ruin, its futility is obvious. Even if the humans involved will be resurrected, they carry the scars of the battle. A new start does not cancel out tragic experience, as the entire series of Riverworld novels indicates. Clemen's relentless determination to avenge himself on John is demeaning to his nature as well as destructive. Clemens himself comes to regret his prosecution of the war during the battle, and to consider that his decision during the Civil War to desert from the Confederate Army was probably wiser. Given the opportunity to kill John personally, Clemens finds that he is too compassionate to kill in cold blood. Nevertheless, Clemens is not above feeling elated when he realizes that John will be drowned in the flooding of the riverboat.

Guilt over his pursuit of John and other actions has haunted Clemens in nightmares where Erik Bloodaxe, whom he has killed in *The Fabulous Riverboat*, pursues him. His guilt intensifies in the battle, since he alone is responsible for it. The final irony of the war occurs when Clemens, rescued by Erik Bloodaxe, now a pacificist with the Church of the Second Chance, dies of a heart attack from fear compounded with overwhelming guilt. Ultimately, Clemens is a tragic victim of his own passion for revenge.

Richard Burton, on the other hand, becomes a successful quest hero in the final section of the novel. However, Burton's success in his quest comes not merely from an individual effort as in *To Your Scattered Bodies Go*, but is attained through teamwork. Burton's completion of the quest has a dual effect: Burton is self-fulfilled and a world is saved. A daring and well-described mountain climbing expedition allows Burton's party to conquer the Dark Tower, where Burton confronts the mysterious Ethical, Loga, who has been a disguised member of his own group. As the Riverworld's secrets are revealed, Farmer presents his own philosophic views about the nature of the soul and the origin of the universe.

Farmer's philosophical outlook in this novel is consistent with that of his other fiction, but it enlarges upon ideas he has presented elsewhere. According to Loga, the Ethical who chooses humanity over scientific experiment, there was a creator in the sense of a First Cause or Source of life; but this being or force is in no sense a personal or responsible god. LIke the idiotic creator of *Venus on the Half-Shell*, it developed life and abandoned it to its own devices. (We should recall that Farmer's god figures who involved themselves with their creations, like Boygur in *Lord Tyger*, are usually insane or inhumane). Even the soul, which Farmer grants a shadowy existence independent of the body, was created not by the creator, but an early race of sentients known simply as the Firsts. (An unresolved paradox is how a race supposedly lacking in self-consciousness could have developed the entity that guarantees self-consciousness; but this is a problem common to evolutionary theories of the origin of conscious life.) Unfortunately, the soul, the *ka* or *wathan*, does not lead a very happy or meaningful existence apart from the body, so the Riverworld experiment was undertaken as a gigantic effort to study the result of resurrecting souls in youthful bodies under controlled conditions.

Farmer leaves open the possibility of a higher kind of existence for the ethically advanced (like Piscator), a state of being in which the wathan goes on to join other highly ethical wathans to form some mystical unity beyond the life of the body. This is not an existence that any of Farmer's major characters is ready to attain, and Farmer is extremely vague about it. In fact, Farmer writes about this mystical state as if it were largely a matter of ethical achievement; not much is said about a mysticism involving contemplative or meditative experience, although such experience might be included under the category of "ethical experience," if the category were stretched.

Broadly speaking, a correct description, or label, for Farmer's philosophic point of view might be "vitalistic humanism" since Farmer places great emphasis on the evolutionary growth of human powers. Despite his tendency to provide naturalistic explanations for spiritual phenomena, Farmer does choose to regard the soul or wathan as non-material, at least so far as the traditional concept of matter is concerned. There are some similarities in Farmer's thought to that of such vitalist thinkers as George Bernard Shaw and Henri Bergson: both transferred some of the traditional concepts of religion, especially Christianity, to a philosophy where a dynamic evolutionary process, and ultimately human intelligence, replaced the idea of a divine creator. Vitalist thinkers usually tend to have a strongly romantic and progressive side to their thought and to view nature in positive terms. Thus Farmer, the sophisticated romancer who insists on the power of the feminine principle or mother goddess, constructs myths consistent with a vitalist point of view.

Whatever one thinks of Farmer's philosophic views, *The Magic Labyrinth* should be valued for ending on a note of drama and intriguing symbolism. It is not simply Burton's intrepidity or Loga's high intelligence that provides the solution to programming the giant computer and restoring the Riverworld to functioning health, but a dream in which Alice Hargreaves receives oracular instruction from Lewis Carroll. There are overtones here of a restoration of lost innocence, as there are also in the encounter with Loga. Loga is revealed as a human who was killed at the age of five and raised by the Ethicals on the "Gardenworld," a pattern that links Loga's concern for humanity with his past as a slaughtered innocent given a special resurrection on an Edenic planet.

This symbolism of the recovery of a lost innocence signifies completion of the quest, not simply for the salvation of the Riverworld, but for the personal quester, Richard Burton. The conclusion of Burton's quest makes more sense on a psychological level if it is read in terms of Jungian symbolism. From this view, Burton ascends from the underworld or labyrinth and conquers the Tower—always a symbol of arcane wisdom and personal achievement in Jung—where he confronts his psychological shadow, Loga, who has mysteriously visited him throughout the epic. The restoration of harmony with the shadow is followed by a revelation from Alice, Burton's *anima*, a delphic suggestion that restores order to Burton's world. Thus, at the end of the novel, Burton has now become a more integrated self, and the Riverworld ceases to be a dark underworld and takes a more comprehensible existence in the light of Burton's knowledge of its origins. Thus, Burton is Farmer's successful quest hero who, in achieving self-integration, also saves a world from extinction. As in the past, Farmer's vision tends to express itself in Jungian symbolism. It is also arguable that the total symbolic form of Burton's epic quest is more important that the philosophic statements presented through Loga.

Another point about Farmer's conclusion should be mentioned here. As *The Magic Labyrinth* ends, Frigate is involved in an enigmatic incident which seems to hint that not all the mysteries of the Riverworld have been fully resolved. Indeed, some will be treated in *Gods of Riverworld*. However, the general shape of Farmer's epic has now been established. Perhaps some of the best possibilities of the Riverworld concept have yet to be realized. But it most be acknowledged that the four novels do constitute a work which in scope, intention, and execution deserves to be regarded as an "epic" in the precise literary sense of the word.

In literary tradition, the epic is a work of considerable stature that deals with a heroic action and presents the author's vision of the origin and destiny of human life. Greek and Latin literary theorists had a set of rules which the author of the epic was supposed to follow and tended to interpret them rather narrowly; but since the Age of Romanticism, of which Farmer is a distant heir, novelists and poets have been more casual about the superficial aspects of epic form. It is now understood that an epic may be written in prose rather than verse, and what constitutes a heroic action is subject to interpretation and change. In *The Iliad* heroism is conceived largely in martial terms, but in *The Odyssey*, heroism means returning home; for Virgil, the heroic action was founding a city; and for Milton, it was confronting temptation. In the nineteenth century, Romantic poets tended to make the epic theme the growth of the imagination, as Wordsworth did, or the imagination's effort to transform the world, as Blake and Shelley did.

All this is fairly well known, and cited here to indicate that Burton's quest to fulfill himself and learn the truth about the Riverworld is clearly an epic theme. The Riverworld novels also present Farmer's vision of the origin and destiny of humanity. If the Riverworld novels are an epic, what then does Farmer think about human destiny? Obviously, Farmer regards the human prospect as a vista of unlimited possibility, awaiting achievement by courageous individuals. To embody his vision, Farmer appropriated the Christian symbol of the resurrected body. Of all the science fiction efforts to suggest the enlarged potential of human life through the use of reason and technology, Farmer's concept of universal resurrection is perhaps the most audacious and imaginative. As a vision of the human hope to transcend the limits of mortality, the Riverworld novels constitute his major bid for literary immortality.

VII
Against the Sun's Darkness:
A Conclusion

Late in 1979, with his audience still awaiting the final novel of the River-world tetralogy, Farmer published *Dark Is the Sun*, one of his best novels. Set on the exhausted Earth fifteen billion years in the future, this book relates the story of another epic journey, the search of Deyv and Vana, a young man and woman from differing tribes who have lost their "soul-eggs," to find themselves and a suitable human destiny. *Dark Is the Sun* depicts a richly detailed primitive world of a very remote future which most consider even beyond imagination. Farmer, however, has envisioned it thoroughly and believably, taking his protagonists through a series of initiations, during which they pass from youth to adulthood. His hero and heroine learn that it is the souls they create through the trials they face, and not the "soul-eggs," which are important. At the end of the novel, Deyv and Vana find a way to another world that promises the possibility of continuing life for humanity. A number of characters accompany them or hinder them on their journey, many of them memorable and two of them very fine achievements: Sloosh, the ageless sentient plant, and Feersh, the blind seeress and witch. Sloosh strikingly embodies the principles of disinterested empirical reason, while remaining a realized personality. Feersh incarnates the oracular power of an unfettered imagination.

Space does not permit a detailed examination of this novel, but it must be recognized as a serene and convincing affirmation. Written at a time when the world worries about a post-industrial dark age from a depletion of energy reserves and other resources, *Dark Is the Sun* is a strong reminder to Farmer's readers that they should not despair of humanity, or surrender to prophets of doom who seem to gloat over the predicted decline of civilized order. For Farmer implies that if the people in *Dark Is the Sun* can continue their struggle with the sun dying out, humanity today certainly ought to find a stronger basis of courage. Set in a future enormously removed, the novel is an affirmation of faith in humanity as it confronts the threat of final extinction.

Dark Is the Sun also might correct some mistaken assumptions about Farmer's thought. Since he sometimes imagines a technology that seems capable of anything, even resurrecting all humanity, some readers may have a tendency to believe that Farmer idolizes technology and considers it the highest good in human life. The world of *Dark Is the Sun*, however, is a world where advanced technology is not even possible; and Farmer sees it as a world where basic human values must be learned and demonstrated once again by his protagonists. *Dark Is the Sun* may be seen as a testament from Farmer which urges today's apprehensive generations to be hopeful and courageous. Its controlled and carefully crafted narrative, its well-realized characters and its memorable vision of the distant future make it one of Farmer's finest achievements.

Farmer followed *The Magic Labyrinth* with another independent novel comparable to *Dark Is the Sun* in richness of characterization, maturity of craftsmanship, and significance of intellectual concern. *The Unreasoning Mask* (1981), written in homage to Herman Melville and his metaphysical search in *Moby-Dick*, is an ambitious statement of Farmer's own evolving religious ideas. Whatever one decides about these, the symbolism in the novel is impressively developed and drawn largely from sources unusual not only for science fiction but for most literature of the English speaking world. Although Farmer's concepts are similar to those of some other post-Darwinian religious thinkers, the novel's symbols and serious tone of quest are memorable, although the book has made no significant impact as yet. One suspects that those readers and critics who have consigned Farmer to a neat label or pigeonhole have either ignored the book or found it baffling. Ultimately, however, the novel may come to be ranked as one of Farmer's best.

Briefly summarized, *The Unreasoning Mask* concerns an agnostic Sufi, Ramstan, who in the distant future commands a star ship named *al-Buraq* and is thrust unexpectedly and unwillingly into a metaphysical quest, not an unusual situation since serious religious quests in literature are often undertaken involuntarily or by accident. Ramstan's quest eventually takes him through a lengthy series of initiations in the "pluriverse" or group of multiple universes that Farmer imagines as making up the total cosmos. There are numerous scientific speculations—including the principle of "alaraf" drive which allows *al-Buraq* to move instantaneously from one point to another, and even to pass through the "gate" dividing one universe from another—but the central theme of the story is Ramstan's search for spiritual enlightenment. Although religiously indifferent at first, Ramstan draws on his Sufi heritage in an attempt to comprehend his encounters with numerous mythic and numinous beings and entities. The symbolism of the novel is indeed rich: there is a cosmic "egg" or *glyfa* which comes into Ramstan's possession and grants him periodic moments of oracular and visionary knowledge; there is a dying sybylline creature called the Webnite who provides ambiguous instructions for the quest; there are three mysterious feminine spirits dressed in green, blue, and black, who resemble the Greek fates; an enigmatic daimonic figure who appears to Ramstan and who seems at times to be Al-Khidr, a messenger from Allah in Islamic mythology; and a sinister and menacing "chaos monster," the *bolg* who must be confronted and overcome as part of Ramstan's final test. This rich body of symbolic material deserves more thorough exploration and analysis than space permits here, but the main outline of Farmer's developing theological position is defined near the end of the novel and may be sketched here.

Put as simply as possible, Farmer's speculative metaphysics postulates a "pluriverse" which is constantly evolving and seeking to become sentient and self-aware, yet is frustrated by actual sentient life and its aberrations such as nuclear war. Humans and other sentients become a kind of "cancer" in the pluriverse by their egotism and by their failure to recognize that their true mission is to help the "pluriverse" become sentient, and not only aware, but to grow to intellectual and moral maturity. Hence the pluriverse creates the *bolg* or "chaos monster" as a protection against the threat it experiences from sentient life when the latter turns destructive and behaves like cancer cells within the body. The real and authentic purpose of all sentient life is to achieve harmony among the species and to envision its true aim as the assistance and education of the evolving pluriverse. By learning this, and by defeating the *bolg*, Ramstan becomes an apostle of enlightenment.

Such a theological position is certainly not orthodox Christianity or Sufism, although it may provide a rational support for the mysticism Farmer was affirming at the time of the completion of the book (in a letter to this author, June 1, 1981, for instance). Nevertheless, certain affinities with other vitalistic theologies and metaphysical theories of "becoming" may be discerned. It is not easy to reconcile Farmer with Hegelian idealism and its dialectics, but the parallels with Bergsonian vitalism and its literary descendants, in Shaw's plays for example, are fairly obvious. Moreover, some readers, especially intellectual Roman Catholics, may very likely be reminded of some of the concepts in the sophisticated evolutionary theology of Teilhard de Chardin.

Whatever one thinks of Farmer's philosophic and religious speculation, however, the importance of *The Unreasoning Mask* should not be overlooked. This austere and finely crafted novel describes one of the more imaginative visionary quests in science fiction. Without a doubt, it is likely to be recognized as one of Farmer's finest speculative works, equal in stature at least to *Dark Is the Sun*. Clearly it is one of Farmer's few novels outside the Riverworld series with a chance to attain the status of a classic of the science fiction genre.

If *The Unreasoning Mask*, for all its strengths, contains few humorous passages and is seldom allowed comic relief, Farmer's next performance is different. *A Barnstormer in Oz* (1982) marks a return to the kind of adventure fiction that Farmer had done so well in the Kickaha books and the Opar series, as well as an exercise in the revision of popular myth so ably achieved with the Tarzan and Doc Savage biographies. In fact, after rewriting the Tarzan myth from a number of different perspectives, and after revising the Doc Savage tales, not to mention parodying Conan Doyle, it was probably inevitable that Farmer would try a revision of the Oz myth as well.

Two of Farmer's favorite worlds of fantasy are Lewis Carroll's Alice books and L. Frank Baum's Oz novels. In resurrecting the real Alice Liddell for the Riverworld novels, Farmer partially repaid his debt to Carroll's books—and in the fifth riverworld novel, *Gods of Riverworld*, he stages his own mad tea party. He had already paid homage to Baum's Oz in *The Lovers* when he named the Edenic planet to which Yarrow travels "Ozagen" literally, "Oz Again." Now, however, Farmer goes much further in *A Barnstormer in Oz* when he provides an adult version of Oz's mythic world: this is truly "Oz Again," re-shaped closer to Farmer's own desire.

A Barnstormer takes Hank Stover, a twenties stunt pilot and former air force officer, through a green cloud to a mysterious world that turns out to be the fabled Oz of Baum's books. Most twenties pilots, however much they might consider themselves rugged and self-reliant individualists, would very likely be immensely shocked by such happenings; but Farmer's hero is merely astonished, for he is actually the son of the original Dorothy whose story provided the inspiration for Baum's first book. Dorothy had emigrated from North Dakota, her actual home, to New York City, where she had abandoned a stenographer's life for the stage; as a chorus girl, she—or rather her shapely legs—had attracted the eye of Lincoln Stover, a scion of Oyster Bay society, and their union had produced Hank. Like many a rebellious young man in the teens and twenties, Hank had become a daredevil (first as a World War I pilot then as a barnstorming carnival entertainer). Such a rebellion parallels that of some famous artists who would have been Hank's contemporaries such as Ernest Hemingway, William Faulkner and Humphrey Bogart. Naturally, this background and the knowlege gained from his mother ensure that Hank does not greet his entrance into fabled Oz with disbelief; but his reaction is by no means a casual yawn.

Before long, Stover meets Oz's real ruler, Glinda the Good, a beautiful white witch with powers that seem supernatural, and another of Farmer's feminine goddess figures. Hopelessly smitten by Glinda's beauty, Stover joins her in a struggle against a malevolent red witch, Erakna, who has long plotted Glinda's overthrow. Soon Hank is also involved in thwarting a secret project of the U.S. Army to sneak through the gate between Earth and Oz with the object of commandeering the latter's jewels and natural resources, a scheme indicative of the amoral and undisciplined Warren G. Harding administration, Farmer implies.

With such premises, A Barnstormer in Oz is likely to strike most readers as highly fanciful, despite numerous efforts of rigorous extrapolation and expositions of scientific logic to justify the marvels of Oz on a rational basis. Farmer postulates immigrations from Earth to Oz in the past; the evolution of sentient animals (the Cowardly Lion and the winged monkeys); special energy beings inhabiting material objects (the Scarecrow); and an arcane science that gives the witches enormous mastery over various kinds of energies and powers (Glinda's and Erakna's special strengths). In addition to all this, Hank and his plane, the Jenny (which at one point becomes sentient herself), sway and glide through a seemingly endless series of adventures to aid Glinda in her intrigues and wars. Despite his hopeless passion for Glinda, Hank marries an ordinary Ozian, Lamblo, who like most of the Ozians is closer to the size of a hobbit than to human stature. He flies into battle with the Tin Woodman aboard the Jenny, prevails against assaults by sentient hawks and winged monkeys, and at the novel's end, saves Glinda's life in her climactic duel with Erakna. Obviously, the novel is essentially a lark for Farmer, an amusing vacation from the demanding efforts of the Riverworld novels and The Unreasoning Mask.

However, for all its inventiveness, the story becomes at times predictable and a little tiresome. Although Hank's skill with a primitive single engine airplane makes him a trickster in the technical sense, he is not given much of a chance to excel as a master of intrigue or tactics. In fact, there are not even many occasions for him to perform extraordinary feats in his plane, actions which might have seemed obligatory in this kind of novel. Regrettably, Hank is Farmer's dullest hero in years, and the book is essentially stolen by an odd pair of scoundrels who travel with him on one adventure, Sharts and Blogo, and by Glinda and the land of Oz itself.

Farmer's Oz is not exactly the earthly paradise and site of initiation trials of Baum's books. Drawing mainly on the first book, The Wizard of Oz—which Baum based on Dorothy's actual adventures, according to Farmer, while the rest were fictional sequels—Farmer transforms Oz into an adult pastoral world which contains violence, ugly deaths, and a good deal of sex in addition to the story's more familiar marvels. Nevertheless, the novel remains in the realm of pastoral or romantic adventure, despite an occasional scene, like the killing of the sentient mouse by the owl, that reminds us of the grimmer realities of our world. Similarly, the clever Glinda is transmuted into a charismatic sex symbol, while remaining an archetypal "good fairy" or white goddess figure.

Farmer can scarcely be blamed for writing such a book, even though there is a touch of self-indulgence about it. Though distinctly a minor work in his canon, *A Barnstormer* is moderately entertaining, and both Oz and the twenties provide a delightful playground for a sophisticated and urbane intelligence like Farmer's. It may be that few besides Farmer could have escaped most of the perils of making an adult version of Oz.

Curiously enough, the danger of self-indulgence once success has been achieved is the central theme of Farmer's most recent novel, *Gods of Riverworld* (1983), which resumes the Riverworld story a few weeks after *The Magic Labyrinth*. In this fifth Riverworld novel we learn that the ambiguous note at the ending of *The Magic Labyrinth* was indeed significant: in many ways the fictional reality of the Riverworld saga becomes shifting and deceptive, and quite different from the impressions given by some of Loga's explanations. Moreover, Loga himself reverts to his nature as a trickster and shadow figure (or daimon) by arranging his apparent murder and disappearing, while setting up an elaborate test for the eight surviving members of Burton's expedition residing in the tower. At his reappearance at the novel's close, Loga's obsessions seem so irrational that Burton pronounces him insane and manages to render him helpless by reducing him to a permanently comatose state.

Loga's test for the eight resurrected terrestrials is a significant one, however. Having gained entrance to the tower and mastery of the enormous computer controlling the ecology of the planet, the eight have in essence acquired godlike powers, not only over their fellow humans, living and dead, but the ability to gratify their own desires. The novel explores the possibilities of how such power will be used. The immediate answer is depressing: as most human beings are likely to do when given enormous resources of power and wealth, the eight squander their gifts on whims and self-indulgent fancies. Each takes a level of the tower and builds his own little dream world. Tom Turpin, the black ragtime pianist, turns his area into a gloriously opulent recreation of St. Louis's red light district at the turn of the twentieth century. Alice asks the computer to manufacture two androids resembling Gladstone and Disraeli who will wait on her, and later makes her quarters into a Lewis Carroll landscape, complete with android replicas of characters from *Wonderland* and *Through the Looking-Glass*. Frigate resurrects a Jewish intellectual lady from the sixties to be his mistress, while transforming his level into a luxurious antebellum Southern mansion surrounded by a prehistoric jungle full of dinosaurs and wooly mammoths. Burton uses the computer to construct his own version of Rabelais's fictional Abbey of Theleme, and also resurrects a beautiful Chinese girl from the T'ang period to be his lover.

Unfortunately, these actions are irresponsible, especially the ill-considered resurrections. Turpin has brought back to life some violent types including one psychopath who attempts to rape Star Spoon, Burton's lover, who carries psychic wounds from abuse in her terrestrial lifetime. Driven to insanity, Star Spoon becomes a murderess and hatches an elaborate plot to destroy everyone living in the tower. As a result, Alice's tea party turns into a mad soiree. Secretly programmed by Star Spoon, Alice's androids suddenly attack the guests and try to murder them. Although Burton, with the aid of some of the others, manages to destroy the androids, this melodramatic violence drives home the lesson that the characters have attempted to evade: they have used their power irresponsibly. In fact, not only have they resurrected persons with a considerable capacity for mischief and destruction, but they have failed to bring back to life some of their loyal comrades who had lost their lives on the quest to reach the tower.

In addition to such mistakes, the characters in *Gods of Riverworld* spend a great deal of time talking about ethics and philosophic theories; but aside from some serious and perceptive comments by Nur, the Sufi moralist, much of the discussion is pointless. The old controversy over free will and determinism is exhumed, for instance, with the conclusion being drawn, not surprisingly, that whether or not humans can prove the existence of free will, they act on the assumption that they do possess freedom. At time, the conversations and debates suggest that the novel is in part a satirical anatomy of the kind Northrop Frye describes in *Anatomy of Criticism* (Princeton, NJ: Princeton U. Press, 1957): that is, a discussion novel or series of imaginary conversations on moral and philosophical issues in which ideas themselves play the role of characters, and the assertion and refutation of concepts becomes a large part of the drama. Here Farmer seems to bring the Riverworld saga somewhat closer to the mode of John Kendrick Bangs' *House-Boat on the Styx*, which he has cited as one of his original inspirations.

Nevertheless, some genuine revelations about the Riverworld universe appear at the close of this finely crafted novel. The concept of a state beyond the body where the soul may journey, on reaching a higher ethical plane, is dismissed by Loga's revelations at the end—at least as far as any scientifically verifiable realm is concerned. Instead, the River Valley is now seen as a kind of purgatorial state, from which those who show ethical advancement will be allowed to graduate by the experimenters from the Gardenworld. One possible reward of ethical progress will be a return to Earth, which is now a world remade by advanced technology into a semblance of its original rich and pastoral self. Thus Farmer holds out the promise not of a mystical realm of spiritual transcendence for his ethical achievers, but instead offers the prospect of a mature earthly paradise or utopia. Yet there is another alternative—one calculated to appeal to restless spirits like Burton. This choice involves the return of humans to one of their original ambitions: the colonization of primitive worlds among the distant stars. For those who choose this way, there will be no repose in the earthly paradise, but a return to hard struggle and heroic effort. Burton sounds the trumpet call of renewed resolution in the closing words of the novel:

> . . . Then Frigate called out, "Is all this rhetorical? Where are *you* going, Dick?
> "You know where," Burton said.
> He waved his hand to indicate the stars.
> (*Gods of Riverworld*, p. 326, Putnam edition).

Here and in the dedication of the book, "To those who won't knuckle under," Farmer asserts once again, as he had in *Dark Is the Sun* and *The Magic Labyrinth*, and in numerous earlier works, the conviction that heroic effort is the most admirable response to the challenge and the responsibility of being human. Perhaps no series by Farmer is ever complete, but *Gods of Riverworld*, the unforeseen fifth book in the saga, comes closer to a true conclusion to the epic.

What final assessment of Farmer's work can be made here? Obviously, this is a difficult question. For one thing, Farmer, though in his early sixties, is still an energetic and ambitious writer at the peak of his powers, with many projects ahead. There will be other Riverworld novels, and Farmer is seriously planning a realistic mainstream novel about himself and his Bohemian friends in the Peoria of the late 1940s.

Another thing that makes Farmer's work hard to evaluate is the fact that so much of the best of Farmer's fiction has been produced in the past dozen years, after Farmer began a full time career in 1969. Certainly any judgment of Farmer's canon would place *Lord Tyger*, *Tarzan Alive*, the Riverworld novels, *Dark Is the Sun*, *The Unreasoning Mask*, and numerous short stories, all produced in this impressive period, at the top of the list. When to these works are added *The Lovers*, *Night of Light* and some short stories from the first two decades, the achievement is solid, without requiring arguments about the merits of other novels or the "World of Tiers" or Opar series.

Selected Bibliography

(NOTE: The most comprehensive bibliography of Farmer's work is George Scheetz's compilation, to be published by Greenwood Press. My work on Farmer is indebted to Scheetz's thoroughness. The primary works here include novels, short story collections, and stories discussed in the text which appear in important anthologies, rather than Farmer collections.)

PRIMARY WORKS

"Sail On! Sail On!" in *Worlds of Maybe*, ed. Robert Silverberg, 1970; repr. NY: Dell, 1974, 77-96. Short story orig. pub. 1952 in *Startling Stories*.

The Green Odyssey. NY: Ballantine, 1957; repr., Boston: Gregg Press, 1978, with an introduction by Russell Letson. Novel.

A Woman A Day. 1960; repr. NY: Berkley, 1980. Novel pub. as *Timestop!* (Lancer, 1968); orig. serialized in *Startling Stories* (1953); expanded into novel in 1960 for Galaxy-Beacon, NY.

Strange Relations. NY: Ballantine, 1960; repr. NY: Avon, 1974. Collection.

The Lovers. NY: Ballantine, 1961; repr. 1972. Expansion of magazine version published in *Startling Stories* in 1952.

The Alley God. NY: Ballantine, 1962. Collection.

Cache from Outer Space. NY: Ace, 1962. Novel. Published in a single volume with *The Celestial Blueprint*.

The Celestial Blueprint and Other Stories. NY: Ace, 1962. Collection.

Fire and the Night. Evanston, IL: Regency, 1962. Novel.

Inside Outside. NY: Ballantine, 1964. Novel.

Tongues of the Moon. 1964; repr. NY: Jove/Harcourt Brace Jovanovich, 1978. Novel expanded from *Amazing Stories* (1961).

Dare. 1965; repr. NY: Berkley, 1979. Novel.

The Maker of Universes. NY: Ace, 1965. Novel.

The Gates of Creation. NY: Ace, 1966. Novel.

Night of Light. 1966; repr. NY: Berkley, 1977. The 1966 version was an expansion of a novel pub. by *Fantasy and Science Fiction*, June 1957.

"Riders of the Purple Wage." in *Dangerous Visions*, ed. Harlan Ellison. 1967; repr. NY: Berkley, 1969, in 3 vols. Farmer's story appears in *Dangerous Visions*, #1, 67-147.

A Private Cosmos. NY: Ace, 1968. Novel.

Flesh. NY: Signet, 1968. Expansion of a novel pub. in *Galaxy* in 1960.

Image of the Beast. 1968; repr. Chicago: Playboy, 1979 (with *Blown*). Novel.

Blown. 1969; repr. Chicago: Playboy, 1979 (as a continuous narrative with

Image of the Beast). Novel.
Feast Unknown, 1969; repr. Chicago: Playboy, 1979. Novel.
Lord Tyger. 1970; repr. NY: Signet, 1972. Novel.
Lord of the Trees and *The Mad Goblin.* NY: Ace, 1970. Two novels in one.
Behind the Walls of Terra. NY: Ace, 1970: Novel.
The Stone God Awakens. NY: Ace, 1970. Novel.
To Your Scattered Bodies Go. 1971; repr. NY: Berkley, 1971. Novel.
The Wind Whales of Ishmael. NY: Ace, 1971. Novel.
The Fabulous Riverboat. 1971; repr. Berkley, 1973. Novel.
Down in the Black Gang and Other Stories. NY: Signet, 1971. Collection.
Tarzan Alive. NY: Doubleday, 1972. Fictional biography.
The Book of Philip Jose Farmer. NY: Daw, 1973. Collection.
Doc Savage: His Apocalyptic Life. 1973; repr. NY, 1975. Fictional biography
    amended and enlarged for Bantam, publisher of Doc Savage series.
The Other Log of Phileas Fogg. NY: Daw, 1973. Novel.
Traitor to the Living. NY: Ballantine, 1973. Novel.
The Adventure of the Peerless Peer. NY: Dell, 1974. Novel.
Hadon of Ancient Opar. NY: Daw, 1974. Novel.
"Greatheart Silver in Showdown at Shootout," in *Weird Heroes,* I, ed. by
    Byron Preiss. NY: Pyramid, 1974, 191-247. First Greatheart Silver story.
Venus on the Half-Shell. NY: Dell, 1975. First serialized in *Fantasy and
    Science Fiction* in 1974; both used Kilgore Trout pseudonym.
Flight to Opar. NY: Daw, 1976. Novel.
Ironcastle. NY: Daw, 1976. Novel by J.H. Rosny appeared in 1922, transl.
    from French and "retold" by Philip Jose Farmer.
Mother Was a Lovely Beast. NY: Pyramid, 1976. Collection ed. by Farmer;
    contains essay on the "feral human" in myth and literature.
The Dark Design. NY: Berkley/Putnam, 1977. Novel.
The Lavalite World. NY: Ace, 1977. Novel.
Time's Last Gift. NY: Ballantine, 1977. Rev. from 1972 Ballantine ed.
Dark is the Sun. NY: Ballantine, 1979. Novel.
Jesus on Mars. Los Angeles: Pinnacle, 1979. Novel.
Riverworld and Other Stories. NY: Berkley, 1979. Collection.
Two Hawks from Earth. NY: Ace, 1979. Expanded and rev. version of
    1966 Belmont ed. (*The Gate of Time*).
The Magic Labyrinth. NY: Berkley/Putnam, 1980. Novel.
Riverworld War: the Suppressed Fiction of Philip Jose Farmer. ed. by
    George Scheetz. Peoria, IL: Ellis, 1980. Condensed version of *Jesus on
    Mars* and five chapters excised from *The Magic Labyrinth.*
"Spiders of the Purple Mage," in *Tales from the Vulgar Unicorn,* ed. by
    Robert Lynn Asprin. NY: Ace, 1980, 5-88. Adventure novelette written
    for "Sanctuary" series.
The Unreasoning Mask. NY: G.P. Putnam's, 1981. Novel.
The Cache. NY: Tom Doherty Assoc., 1981. Contains *The Long Warpath*
    orig. pub. as *The Cache from Outer Space* (NY: Ace, 1965), and two short
    stories, "They Twinkled like Jewels," and "Rastignac the Devil."
Father to the Stars. NY: Pinnacle, 1981. Five Carmody stories.
The Purple Book. NY: Tom Doherty Assoc., 1982. Contains "Riders of the
    Purple Wage," and other stories.
A Barnstormer in Oz. NY: Berkley, 1982. Novel.
Gods of Riverworld. NY: G.P. Putnam's, 1983. Novel.

SECONDARY SOURCES

Bangs, John Kendrick. *A House-Boat on the Styx*. NY: Harper, 1895; repr. Louisville, KY: Lost Cause Press, 1973.

Baring-Gould, William S., *Sherlock Holmes of Baker Street*. NY: Bramhall House, 1962.

Bettelheim, Bruno, *The Uses of Enchantment: The Meaning and Importance of Fairy Tales*. 1976; reprinted, New York: Vintage Books, 1977.

Campbell, Joseph. *The Hero with a Thousand Face*. 1949: Second Edition, repr. Princeton, NJ: Princeton Univ. Press, 1972.

DeLaszlo, Violet S., ed., *The Basic Writings of C.G. Jung*. NY: Random House, 1959.

Eckley, Grace. "Waking the *Wake* in Farmer's 'Wage,'" *Farmerage* I (October 1978), 10-17.

Farwell, Byron. *Burton*. NY: Holt Rinehart Winston, 1963.

Fiedler, Leslie. *Love and Death in the American Novel*. 1960; rev. ed., 1966; repr. NY: Dell, 1966.

_____. "Thanks for the Feast," in *The Book of Philip Jose Farmer*. NY: Daw, 1973, 232-239; orig. pub. in Los Angeles *Times*, April 23, 1972.

Frye, Northrop. *Anatomy of Criticism*. Princeton, NJ: Princeton Univ. Press, 1957.

_____*The Secular Scripture: A Study of the Structure of Romance*. Cambridge, MA: Harvard Univ. Press, 1976.

Graves, Robert. *The White Goddess*. 1948; amended and enlarged ed., 1966; repr. NY: Farrar Straus and Giroux, 1973.

Jannone, Claudia. "*Venus on the Half-Shell* as Structuralist Activity." *Extrapolation* XVII (May 1976), 1964.

Letson, Russell. "The Faces of a Thousand Heroes: Philip Jose Farmer." *Science-Fiction Studies* IV (March 1977), 35-41.

_____. "The Worlds of Philip Jose Farmer," *Extrapolation* XVIII (May 1977), 124-130.

Lupoff, Richard. *Edgar Rice Burroughs: Master of Adventure*. 1965; rev. ed., NY: Ace, 1968.

Platt, Charles. "Philip Jose Farmer," in *Dream Makers: The Uncommon People Who Write Science Fiction* (Interviews by Charles Platt). NY: Berkley, 1980, 121-132.

Pringle, David. "Philip Jose Farmer," in *The Science Fiction Encyclopedia*, ed. by Peter Nicholls. Garden City, NY: Dolphin, 1979, 217-218.

Rottensteiner, Franz. "Playing Around with Creation: Philip Jose Farmer," *Science-Fiction Studies* I (Fall 1973), 94-98.

Scheetz, George. *Philip Jose Farmer: A Bibliography*. Unpublished manuscript scheduled for publication by Greenwood Press.

Scholes, Robert and Rabkin, Eric S. *Science Fiction: History, Science, Vision*. NY: Oxford Univ. Press, 1977.

Shah, Idries. *The Sufis*. 1964; repr., Garden City, NY: Anchor, 1971.

Wymer, Thomas. "Speculative Fiction, Bibliographies, and Philip Jose Farmer," *Extrapolation* XVIII (December 1976), 59-73.

_____. "The Trickster as Artist," in *Voices for the Future*, vol. II, ed. Thomas Clareson (Bowling Green, OH: Bowling Green Popular Press, 1979), 34-55.

Index